Yorkshire Pie

Yorkshire Pie

A confection of remarkable tales from God's own county.

Ivor Smullen

Fort Publishing

First published in 2001 by Fort Publishing Ltd, Old Belmont House,
12 Robsland Avenue, Ayr, KA7 2RW.

Front Cover design by Justin Wilson, 01560 700208
Back Cover illustrations by D. Shaw, 0141 248 7584

Cover graphics by Paul McLaughlin, 01387 810612

Printed by Bell and Bain Ltd., Glasgow

Typeset in 10.5pt Sabon by Senga Fairgrieve, 0131 658 1763

ISBN 0-9536576-5-5

A catalogue record for this book is available from the British Library.

Contents

Acknowledgements

For their help in my researches for this anthology of curious Yorkshire people, places and events, I would like to thank Catherine Hamilton, Collections and Access Officer, Sheffield Industrial Museums Trust; the Local Studies Departments of Bradford Central, Sheffield Central, Scarborough, Leeds Central, Beverley, Huddersfield, York Central, Castleford, Pontefract and Hull Central Libraries; Dr D.J. Marchant, Museums Registrar, East Riding of Yorkshire Council; Michelle Petyt, Assistant Curator of Social History, York Castle Museum; the Johnson Consultancy Ltd, Sheffield; the *Yorkshire Evening Post* Library; the staff of Hughenden Manor, Bucks; Frank Flaherty, General Manager, Majestic Hotel, Harrogate; Dee Atkinson and Harrison, Auctioneers, Beverley; Michelle Roberts, Marketing Officer, Theatre Royal, York; Robin Compton of Newby Hall, Ripon; Jackie Hill of The Saltburn Smugglers, Saltburn; Trebor Bassett Ltd, London; Robert Thompson's Craftsmen Ltd, Kilburn; *Country Life* Picture Library; the Social Sciences Section of Manchester Central Library; *History Today* magazine; and Rob Swain, director, and Liz Wilson of the marketing department of the Harrogate Theatre.

Introduction

SOME 80 YEARS AGO, an editor of the *Barnsley Chronicle* kept in an office drawer a packet of pepper and a pickaxe handle with which to repel outraged readers. Some would argue that he was the archetypal Yorkshireman: opinionated, aggressive and intolerant. This is certainly a reputation the county's citizens, perhaps with tongues firmly in cheeks, have delighted in bolstering. There are Yorkshiremen today who would strike fear into the hearts of persons unfortunate enough to hail from more effete sections of the country. You would not tread on Geoffrey Boycott's toes or sneer at Sir Bernard Ingham's tie with impunity. One of England's most terrifying historical characters was a true Yorkshireman, William Shaw, proprietor of Bowes Academy, which, following a personal visit, Dickens transformed into Dotheboys Hall, with Shaw retaining his initials in the new guise of Wackford Squeers.

On the other hand, it may be claimed that many of the fearsome stories told about Yorkshiremen (and their mothers) derive from their flat, blunt vowels, which suggest a refusal to admit error, and allow none of the equivocations of, say, a whining Cockney. A journalist of my acquaintance once interviewed that great son of Bradford, J.B. Priestley. Within minutes of my friend's arrival, the author threw up his hands and declaimed: 'People say I'm rude. Nothing could be further from the truth.' He had no pickaxe handle in his drawer, so perhaps he was telling the truth.

Yorkshire is, nonetheless, the home of single-minded and assertive persons and pub pontificators. But also of admirably tenacious people who achieve success no matter what obstacles (or how many southerners) stand in their way. In their ranks we find Jo Thompson, daughter of a Co-op butcher in Batley, who became the feisty chief executive of Camelot, and reclaimed the National Lottery licence after a formidable tussle with Sir Richard Branson. Boasting similar grit and determination is Sir Kenneth Morrison, of Bradford, who began his working life delivering Christmas parcels and ended up one of the nation's great supermarket tycoons. Morrison refuses to go to London to present his financial reports, arguing that 'you can get away with it if you are a character'. When he discloses that outsiders 'put us down as Yorkshire puddings', he grins. His success is the best answer to such supercilious jibes.

Another county icon is the former £3-a-week *Yorkshire Evening Post* typist, Barbara Taylor Bradford, whose Yorkshire parents instilled in her the compulsion to excel, and who thus became a blockbusting novelist (with the odd distinction of having her face plastered on Caribbean postage stamps). A namesake, William Bradford, though now largely forgotten, helped change history's course. Born at Austerfield, near Doncaster, in 1590, he became a Puritan at the age of 12, seven years later joined a group of noncomformists who migrated to Holland in search of religious freedom, and finished up organising an expedition of about 100 pilgrims to the New World. He became a colonial governor and historian, ruled firmly and wisely, and displayed tact (not universally considered a Yorkshire virtue) in dealing with the people we now call Native Americans.

The Yorkshireman's spirit of individuality has led, in some quarters, to demands for the setting up of the region's own parliament, on the lines of those in Scotland and Wales. Meanwhile, his sturdy character has produced a group of extraordinary citizens, some of whom are described in the following pages, along with the often unusual places and surroundings in which they lived. To the world outside Yorkshire's borders they are, it is true, curiosities. To themselves, they are just plain folk.

Ivor Smullen
2001

CHAPTER I

STRANGE FOLK

FATTISM

A preacher proposed to visit the village of Cropton, near Whitby. Not too pleased with the prospect, a local churchwarden issued a public warning:

> A man will be coming to Cropton soon who calls himself 'The Yorkshire Evangelist'. He is a great, fat, overfed fellow, and I want to give the Cropton folk some information about him. He has an enormous appetite. He ate at Westerdale three of Mr Cass Smith's best show sheep in one week, and so he [Mr Smith] could not exhibit at the agricultural shows any more. At Farndale, in one week, he ate a fat bullock and all Sally Ford's preserves. He wants three eggs to breakfast every day and a big ham every three days.

The warning merely served to make the parishioners eager to see this great wonder of nature. They flocked to the chapel, even from neighbouring villages, and many were converted.

❄ ❄ ❄

STAINLESS AND PEERLESS

Anyone who was a pupil at the Crookes endowed church school in Sheffield in the 1920s will remember Arthur Clifford Baines, one of the teachers. He was a stern disciplinarian and had the disconcerting habit of disappearing early in the afternoon to catch a train to Manchester. There, in a local studio, he would display another side of his personality, that of a broadcasting comedian. In later years, at the height of his fame, he performed on radio and the music-halls as Stainless Stephen, in a voice resembling that of a disconsolate frog. His trade mark was his insistence on speaking the punctuation of his script and then parodying his apparent obsession. A line from a wartime script ran: 'We're a great race, the British. All comrades, semi-colon. All shoulders to the wheel, semi-quaver. We'll carry on until the Axis turns semi-turtle, and Hitler asks for a full stop, exclamation mark.'

Born in 1892, Baines joined the Lancashire and Yorkshire Regiment during the First World War, rising to the rank of sergeant-major, and being twice wounded. It was at an Army sig-nallers' course that he conceived the idea of 'audible punctuation'. When his brother joined him in the Forces, the two wrote jokes and sketches which they performed at unit concerts. After the war Baines resumed his former teaching profession, but, after a successful appearance in a show promoted by the Sheffield Comrades' Association in the Temperance Hall, he was persuaded by a pianist on the bill to become a semi-professional comic. He played under the name Arthur Clifford and was also in great demand as an after-dinner speaker. After broadcasting from London's 2LO station (which preceded the BBC), he decided, at thirty-four, to become a full-time comic. He was inspired to adopt the stage name Stainless Stephen when he saw a suit of armour in a Sheffield shop. He persuaded a local firm to make him a steel waistcoat, which they presented to him on the Sheffield Empire stage. Later sartorial additions were a stainless steel hat-band, waistcoat buttons that lit up, and a revolving bow-tie, also luminous. By 1931 he was topping the bill at Barnsley's Theatre Royal and a year later was voted top radio comedian in a daily newspaper poll.

During the Second World War he entertained troops at home bases and in Burma. With tongue in cheek he ruefully confessed he had never managed to achieve his ambition of playing the harpsi-chord at the Albert Hall. When a reader's letter in the *Daily Mirror* in 1966 reported, with some exaggeration, that he had died six years earlier, he wrote to point out that, having retired from the stage in 1952, he had been living in Kent as a gentleman farmer 'raising nothing but my hat'. His letter was signed 'Stainless Stephen (semi-solvent)'. He in fact died five years later at the age of seventy-nine.

❆ ❆ ❆

A MACHINE FOR THE LOST HORIZON

The Revd Norman Driver gave the world the first machine that could type the Tibetan alphabet: an extraordinary achievement for a Yorkshireman by any standards.

A former French-polishing apprentice at Bradford, Driver joined the Moravian Church, a Protestant religious order founded in the eighteenth-century. Appointed a missionary, he was sent in 1933 to Leh, an Indian town linked by road to Tibet. After the partition of India and the creation of Pakistan, Driver and his wife disappeared. The headmistress of the Pudsey school where their two daughters were being educated contacted a former Hull East MP, Lord Calverley, through whose journalist contacts the Drivers were eventually traced.

On his return to England, the clergyman set himself the task of manufacturing a Tibetan typewriter that would help spread the Gospel and facilitate the work of the churches in what is known as 'the roof of the world'. No such machine at that time existed, and though the Americans had a typewriter that could have been adapted, it was electric, of little use in a country where electricity was in short supply.

Driver's task was complicated by the fact that Tibetan script is written both horizontally and vertically, with dots between syllables. Each dot requires, in typewriter terms, a half-space. In the course of his researches Driver came across an old Olympia typewriter with, of all oddities, a half-space key. But more importantly, his team found an Urdu machine with different spaces for different letters: the answer, once adapted, to his prayers. The replacement of the Urdu by Tibetan characters was a colossal but not impossible job. It cost a mere £400.

AGONY UNCLE

Job Senior, a.k.a. The Hermit of Ilkley Moor, lived, through force of circumstances, in an outsized kennel. He had been happy leading a blameless life as a nineteenth-century singer, soothsayer and weather forecaster. But his fate was sealed when he married a woman twenty years his junior and with a well-appointed cottage at Burley Woodhead, near Ilkley, which he believed would provide him with a comfortable home for the rest of his life. Unfortunately, she died soon after the marriage, and her relatives were so furious when they learned that Job would inherit the cottage, that they broke in, removed all the furnishings they considered rightfully theirs, and then razed it to the ground. All that Job found when he returned home was a heap of shattered stones. With the debris he built a small, kennel-like shelter so tiny he had to creep in on all fours. When a storm was brewing, he tied ropes round the structure to ensure it remained in one piece, and when gales ripped the roofs off village houses, his own residence survived unscathed. Sightseers flocked to Burley Woodhead to see the ragged recluse tilling his potato patch. He would tour the district singing for other food, becoming a familiar figure in his multi-patched coat and trousers, and, on his matted, uncut hair, a battered hat from which dangled a pipe on a string. Straw tied around his legs helped him keep warm, and, as he wore no socks, overflowed from his wooden clogs. A rheumatic, he walked with the aid of two sticks. Despite his appearance, he was regarded as an adviser on personal problems, warning lovestruck young men not to marry. (After all, look what happened to him.) Taken ill with cholera when out walking, he sheltered in a hay-barn and was quickly removed to a workhouse, where he died. He is commemorated by the Hermit Inn, at Burley Woodhead, which boasts a sign bearing his alleged portrait.

THE BOUNTY MAN

Benjamin Blaydes of Hull was the man who built the most notorious ship in British naval history, the *Bounty*. His family had been in the shipbuilding business for two centuries, and he himself was laden with honours. He held such offices as Governor of the Port, Sheriff and (three times) Mayor of Hull. He it was who instigated the Hull – Hamburg run. With ships rarely out of his mind, he would take regular walks along the waterfront to watch clippers disgorging or welcoming passengers. On one of these vessels, it was reported, people and pigs occupied the best cabin.

Benjamin lived in Blaydes House, an elegant residence boasting a four-pillared portico and marble front step. (In 1999 Hull University announced that it planned to convert the house into an international research centre devoted to the history of seafaring in general and the *Bounty* in particular.)

All in all, Blaydes had an enviable position in the town where he lived and worked. It did, however, seem to go to his head. One significant story tells of the day Blaydes, who had an unusually swarthy complexion, was standing on the dockside when a party of gipsies seeking a ferry across the Humber approached him. Quite amiably, one of them asked if he would like to accompany them across the river. Puzzled, Blaydes asked why. The gipsy replied that, because of the colour of the gentleman's skin, he assumed 'you are one of us'. Blaydes cleared up the misapprehension by grabbing the man's throat and trying to strangle him, until his victim was fortunate enough to be rescued by passers-by. Hardly the sort of behaviour you would expect from a distinguished citizen.

Some might argue that Blaydes's disposition exerted a malign influence on the ships he built, and that the mutiny on the *Bounty* was predestined. The *Bounty*, in fact, was not the only Blaydes ship that met with disaster. Another vessel built by the firm was the *Ardent*, a 1,376-tonner with seventy guns: the largest naval vessel built on the Humber in the eighteenth-century. When Blaydes was experiencing a fallow period, the Hull MP William Wilberforce (the slave trade abolitionist) pleaded in Parliament for more commissions for the Blaydes yard. The chief Navy spokesman retorted that soon after the *Ardent* was fitted out, her rotten timbers had to be repaired, and in 1782, near Havana, she sank in a calm sea on a fine summer's day. The spokesman suggested caution. Blaydes also owned the *British Queen*, a whaler lost at sea seven years after her maiden voyage.

The *Bounty* was built in Blaydes's yard in 1784. She was originally intended to be a coal-ferrying merchant ship called the *Bethia*, until the Admiralty bought her for £2,600, fitted her out to carry bread-fruit trees from Tahiti to the West Indies, renamed her the *Bounty*, and placed her under the captaincy of William Bligh.

Eight years after Bligh arrived home following the mutiny, he himself came to Hull as commander of the Humber Guardship, HMS *Director*, from which he mapped the lower part of the estuary. Blaydes left a curious will. To a local mariner's wife he bequeathed a Hull pub whose sign bore a painting of a ship, leading to subsequent speculation that she could have been a trusted servant or, more interestingly, a former mistress. His oddest bequest was to his two sons: half a ship to each of them.

❄ ❄ ❄

SOOTHING THE SAVAGE BREAST

There was a time when, if one saw a donkey dancing in the street, it could safely be assumed that this was Billy Commons in disguise. His outfit was reputedly so realistic that a genuine ass, grazing on moorland and happening to see Billy pass by, was moved to chase him down the road. Billy was the leader of a group of madcap musicians from Morley, near Leeds, one of several outlandishly garbed comic bands whose members often sported painted faces. They marched along the streets of Yorkshire until the late 1930s, raising cash for charities and beer-money for themselves. One of their favoured instruments was the kazoo, nicknamed the tommy talker. They also played whistles, combs-and-paper, concertinas, metal teapots (with spouts flattened into mouthpieces) and various instruments made of cardboard and thin sheet tin. An aggregation from the Hunslet district of Leeds was known alternatively as the

Wiffum Waffum Band and the Nanny-Goat Lancers. As they played 'The Death of Nelson' standing in a wagon, each in turn fell down to disappear into the wagon's bottom. At a comic band contest, the Jungle Band won with this instrumental piece not because they were better musicians but 'because their conductor died better'. At such contests, musicians were firmly forbidden to play normal musical instruments, and they wore anything from leopard-skins to uniforms made from painted sugar-bags.

Brass bands, however, have played the most significant role in Yorkshire's musical life. On Boxing Day, a makeshift band in Hemingbrough, near Selby, would make the rounds of all the village houses and outlying farms to play carols, in return for ducks, geese, rounds of cheese and the odd glass of rum. In Cleckheaton a brass bandsman would play rousing tunes on a trombone to lure crowds at markets and fairs to a tooth-puller operating from a coal merchant's cart. The trombone would drown patients' screams.

Competitiveness between bands led to extraordinary behaviour. The records reveal cases of contestants who were not above ingenious skulduggery in their efforts to steal a march (no pun intended) on their rivals. Batley Old Band players sealed their instruments with soap to prevent 'wind loss' before a Manchester event in 1896.

Others did their utmost to damage the playing capabilities of their opponents' instruments by such practices as secretly dropping soft, chewed toffees into the tubes. When a West Riding band held a practice session in a stable, a bribed stable-boy tipped a bag of soot, through rat-holes, over the conductor's head. There could even be disastrous rivalry among individual members of a single band. When, not too many years ago, some of the players in the Sellers Engineering Band of Huddersfield played 'Land of Hope and Glory', others, with equal fervour, struck up 'Scotland the Brave'. The conductor blamed a handful of malcontents in the trombone and cornet sections.

The enthusiasm of performers could not always be taken as read. A band representing the village of Kirkbymoorside was deputed to play at the unseemly hour of six in the morning. Worse, the performance was to be given from a church tower. With their instruments, music stands and music sheets, the bandsmen were pushed, pulled and cajoled up ladders through the bell-chamber and out of a trap-door onto the tower's gentle slope. In the centre stood a flagpole and around the assembly was a battlemented parapet. All highly atmospheric. But not, alas, for two acrophobic bandsmen who flung their arms around the flagpole and declined to budge. When the baton-wielder remonstrated that they had nought to fear, one of the men not only insisted that he would not be moved, but claimed that the bandmaster's knees were knocking efficiently enough to beat time. The band eventually played a little ditty that ran, 'Up in the sky, ever so high, sailing in my balloon', applauded by citizens in nightshirts and nightcaps down below.

Until women were permitted to join brass bands, there were stories of the havoc band membership could wreak on marital life. One bandsman was said to make his wife sleep on the sofa so that he could snuggle up beside his big bass and 'keep it warm'.

The Yorkshire finalists at a recent Royal Albert Hall competition were the Carlton Main Frickley Colliery Band, whose chairman recalled practising the soprano cornet at the age of six in the colliery's canary house, a 12ft square, windowless room. 'We knew only one piece, *Abide With Me* and a C scale,' he said. 'The canaries didn't like it much.'

❄ ❄ ❄

COASTAL CHARACTERS

The scores of miles of Yorkshire's often rugged coastline spawned a variety of strange characters. Among these were egg-snatchers, who lowered themselves down perilous cliffs to reach birds' eyries. An American visitor penned a graphic account of his meeting with a typical Victorian snatcher in the Flamborough area. The latter was accompanied by two male assistants and his wife, 'a strong, muscular woman with an arm as brawny as that of the village blacksmith'. He admitted having suffered many accidents during his forty-year pilfering career: a broken arm, teeth knocked out and a cracked skull more than once. Here is the snatcher preparing for his descent: 'First he rolls down the cliff a stout rope, which is fixed to an iron stake; next he affixes round each thigh a hempen loop, which he calls his breeches.' Lowered by his wife and assistants down the 300ft almost perpendicular cliff, he excites the birds: 'The kittiwakes hover round and round him, calling, "Git away, git away." The auk swoops down as if it would attack him, but only utters a hoarse, "Ur, ur, ur, ur," which sounds like a smothered curse, and then drops into the ocean beneath, while a few half-fledged birds, unable to fly, call, "Ullock, ullock." ' The climber now plants his feet firmly against the rocks, sways back and forth, swings off the cliff for several feet, comes back with a thud, loosens a mass of rock, crawls a short way along a ledge, picks the eggs and drops them into his satchel.

Many of the coastal fishermen and their families were prone to bizarre superstitious practices. When a smack from Staithes had a run of bad luck, the fisherwives would gather at midnight and, in deep silence, kill a pigeon, extract its heart, stick it full of pins, and burn it over a charcoal fire. Another ploy was to keep the first fish caught after a long, unproductive period, and burn it as a sacrifice to the Fates. Fishermen regarded all four-footed animals as unlucky, especially pigs. If, while they were stowing their nets into a boat, somebody incautiously mentioned a pig, they would stand stock-still, and might even refuse to do any fishing at all that day. If, on his way to his boat, a fisherman met a woman, even his own wife or daughter, he considered this an ill omen. For this reason, whenever a woman saw a fisherman approaching her on his way to work, she would turn her back on him.

As early as 1539, some Staithes fishermen were called to serve in the Navy. Throughout the eighteenth century they were frequently visited by members of the notorious Whitby-based press-gang. Thus many of the sailors who fought at the Battle of Trafalgar hailed from Staithes, while numerous other local men spent years in French prison-camps during the Napoleonic wars. It was a Staithes sea-captain who commanded the first vessel to sail into the Japanese port of Yokohama after it was opened to foreign trade. In more recent years Staithes men have commanded large ocean-going vessels.

But the most talked-of mariner of the Yorkshire coastal regions was born to a farm labourer in the village of Marton. He was christened James and survived the handicap of having to listen many times, in his early years, to one of his century's most awful puns. When his father had left his own home as a boy, he allegedly received from his mother the blessing, 'God send you grace!' James's father frequently made the tiresome observation that, as he had married a Cleveland woman named Grace, his mother's prayer had been clearly answered.

At sixteen, James himself was apprenticed to a Staithes haberdasher, spending his leisure hours making short trips in a fishing coble. One day a woman customer gave him a new shilling. Attracted by its shine, he pocketed it, replacing it with one of his own coins. But the shopkeeper called him a thief. So the lad quit, took to a seafaring life, and is now known to history as Captain James Cook, explorer extraordinary.

A rather more apocryphal tale concerns that well-known mediaeval crook, Robin Hood, who, when the military were making things hot for him in Nottingham, is said to have headed for Yorkshire, and found an ideal refuge in a bay wherein nestled a fishing hamlet. Sometimes, he and his men would sail, in fishing-boats, the six miles to Whitby, then a mere village. One day, after dining with the Abbot of Whitby, the latter asked if Robin would mind demonstrating his shooting prowess. Robin thereupon climbed onto the Abbey roof with his men and loosed several arrows in the direction of the village. They fell on each side of a lane a mile from the Abbey. The astounded abbot reportedly set up a memorial to this feat on the very spot. As for the fishing hamlet which the master criminal transformed into a robbers' hideaway, this became known as Robin Hood's Bay.

If the Yorkshire coast was good for Robin's health, it did no harm, either, a few centuries later, to a lady known as Peg Pennyworth. An inordinately wealthy woman, Peg was, during the eighteenth century, one of the most frequent visitors to Scarborough. She hated buying goods on credit, and whenever she made a purchase, would send a footman along with the cash. This was usually one penny, as she was not overly extravagant. Once she bought several live eels, and stuffed them into her pockets before stepping with a woman friend into a coach. When the creatures slipped out and began slithering along the coach floor (to her companion's horror), she simply gathered them up and continued her journey. She lived to be 103, and you can't get much healthier than that.

THE HECKLER

For John Kemble, the distinguished eighteenth-century actor, it was a night that, in later years, he would rather not remember. He was playing at York Theatre Royal where audiences were renowned for their truculence towards performers who did not, in their view, come up to snuff. Kemble's role was that of Teribazus in a play called *Zenobia* and a lady in one of the boxes did not like the way he went about it. As a Victorian historian of the theatre later put it:

> She . . . openly and loudly proclaimed her dislike to Mr Kemble's style, and greeted the best scenes of the play with screams of laughter. Mr Kemble was a little annoyed at such pointed rudeness, so in the last scene he conveyed looks of disdain, of which he was capable, to the lady, which looks were as scornfully returned with reiterated bursts of laughter. On the repeated repetition of such injurious and indelicate behaviour, Mr Kemble abruptly stopped, and when called upon by the audience to 'Go on!, go on!', he, with great gravity and a pointed bow to the stage-box, said he was ready to proceed with the play as soon as *that lady* had finished her conversation . . . The audience was roused, and in general hissed the lady out of the theatre. She could not bear such an unexpected insult . . .

Her retaliation verged on the incredible. Among the audience, she knew, were officers of the North Riding Militia, who, unaccountably, she numbered among her admirers. She thus issued orders to them, the result of which was a confrontation between

Kemble and the officers in the manager's rooms. The soldiers' manner was peremptory and cold. The handsome Kemble, on the other hand, was 'cool, deliberate, determined, and not to be alarmed by threats or numbers'. He did, however, agree to make a reconciliatory statement from the stage. But when he made his appearance, the pit and the gallery cried, 'No apology! No apology!' Kemble insisted on silence and then began to make a statement in defence of his profession. This was not what the army officers had expected, and they called out: 'We want none of your conversation or jabbering here. It is very imprudent and impertinent. Talk no more, sir, but instantly ask pardon!' The disdainful Kemble retorted: 'Pardon? No sirs! Never!' and left the stage amid bursts of applause from his supporters. The lady, in her turn, left the theatre 'pale and sick'.

✳ ✳ ✳

HOCUS POCUS

A couple who had taken over a Bradford city-centre restaurant in the 1980s were clearing junk out of the attic when they found a striking, Egyptian-style painting on the wall. They also discovered an inscription above the door. It was a strange motto that began:

> Wise Men
> Holding Wisdom Highest
> Scorn Delights more false than fair . . .

The attic, it turned out, was nothing less than the long-lost Yorkshire temple of followers of The Golden Dawn, a weird and now virtually forgotten cult. Known as the Temple of Horus, it seems to have attracted largely middle-class, well-educated people who ought to have known better and probably shared a childish penchant for secrets and silly symbols. It flourished between 1887 and 1923, and the Bradford temple in Godwin Street was the largest in the provinces, with fifty-seven initiates listed between 1888 and 1896, among them a doctor rejoicing in the name Bogdan Jastrzebski Edwards.

The temple was formally consecrated by Samuel Mathers, a self-styled mystic and son of a Cockney clerk, at a ceremony in a local hotel whose landlord joined the Order but resigned when he was declared bankrupt. An honorary member of the Horus Temple was a cleric, the Revd William Ayton, who, a few years earlier, had been swindled by another odd brotherhood, but was seemingly not put off by the experience.

The activities of the Golden Dawn were daft but harmless. Members pursued elaborate rituals which it is rather difficult to describe in full. This task occupied four volumes and more than 1,000 pages in a gargantuan volume published in the United States around half a century ago. It is, however, possible to give a flavour of the proceedings. There was the predictable incense-burning, fooling with pentagrams and hexagrams, and muttering of incantations, while all concerned liked to dress up in fancy clothes. One Temple officer, for instance, wore a white cassock, a red cloak, a yellow and white Egyptian headdress and (most fearful of all) yellow shoes. He also carried a multi-coloured sceptre, a white lamp, a brazier and a candle, but presumably not all at once. Another essential item of equipment was a wand with a lotus flower screwed into one end. One tip was white, the other black, the latter considered 'the most suitable for invocation, but with the greatest caution'. Today you can buy this sort of thing at any good magic shop.

About one Temple ritual there was a certain hide-and-seek element. It involved a senior official being concealed behind a curtain which, at intervals, he would part slightly to reveal his hands making 'a sign' with a torch. At his initiation ceremony a new convert would wear a black robe, with a chain round his neck, and his hands, like those of a movie hero *in extremis*, tied behind his back. The poor fellow was forced to listen without yawning to a lecture on the virtues of humility, and had to swear not to divulge to the outer and more ignorant world the secrets of the cult's 'magical implements' and its involvement in such activities as divination by tarot cards, other forms of clairvoyance and astral projection (otherwise known as out-of-body experiences). Meanwhile, the

Temple chief would lie cosily in a coffin in his full regalia with his arms crossed over his breast and simultaneously holding a crook: no mean feat.

Unhappily, meetings at the Temple (generally on Sundays) were not as frequent as those in London, as members lived all over the north of England and often found travelling difficult despite their magical powers. But, in or out of the Temple, most never forgot their loyalty to the cult. When writing to fellow-devotees, for instance, they were instructed to stick their stamps on the envelopes with the monarch's head facing upwards: an equivalent of the secret handshake.

One London-based official of the cult was Annie Horniman, from the famous tea family. In 1892 she came to Yorkshire to discipline two allegedly unruly members of the Temple. One was a Brother Firth who, when asked to act as temple auditor, 'refused rudely and disrespectfully', and, firmly sitting down, exclaimed, 'I shan't!' It was even suggested that he had laughed at some of the Temple rituals and poured scorn on the art of astrology, which the cult held sacred. The other troublesome member was a Brother Harrison, who, at tea in a semi-public room, spoke as if the Temple ceremonies 'were only foolish mummeries in his eyes'. The spread of such sentiments presumably led, eventually, to the demise of this wondrous cult.

❄ ❄ ❄

GASLIGHT MUSIC

The history of wireless has produced no artefact stranger than the gas radio, produced shortly before the Second World War. This was a time when, for many people, electricity was a domestic luxury, while radios that operated off cumbersome accumulators had to be recharged every week. Henry Milnes, who ran a radio firm in Bingley, decided that what was needed was a cheap and easy-to-use radio for listeners still living in gas-lit homes.

Milnes produced sets that contained a thermo-electric generator powered by the gas supply in the home. Inside the generator were two rows of forty tiny gas jets designed to heat platinum thermocouples. Within a minute of the jets being lit, the generator developed full power and supplied a steady stream of electricity to the radio. The jets were carefully regulated, the gas rate controlled by a governor incorporated within the unit, which came in three sizes (4, 6.4 and 8 watts). Instead of plugging into the mains, the radio owner simply turned on the gas.

A gas radio did not take long to warm up. The time that elapsed between the lighting of the jets and the sound of Henry Hall's orchestra filtering into the parlour was shorter than with an electric radio.

Milnes put the radios on sale shortly before the outbreak of war, when Britain boasted some nine million homes with receivers. His sets cost just £4. A four-watt model ran for an hour on four cubic feet of gas, with a guaranteed working life of 5,000 hours. The radios were also sold abroad. A booklet Milnes produced for their owners claimed they were more dependable than orthodox sets, since 'generating stations can break down but the gas supply never fails.' Repairs being expensive, instruction sheets warned owners to check their generators regularly to avoid the risk of 'serious damage' if anything went wrong.

Clearly interested in the potential for increasing gas consumption, the Severn Valley Gas Corporation announced that it was 'watching developments closely'. Gas company showrooms were among Milnes's best customers, their managers possibly considering that radios demonstrated the versatility of gas more dramatically than conventional cookers.

At the end of the war, almost every British home had electricity. The gas companies had lost interest in the gas radio, and it slipped into oblivion. Milnes now invented an alkaline accumulator and horn-type loudspeakers for the high-fidelity relay of the *Music While You Work* programmes broadcast from the nation's factories.

In a letter to the *Radio Times* in 1953, a former gas radio owner confirmed that its reception had been 'of a very high quality' but added that gas consumption 'was considered rather excessive'.

In the same year Milnes's wife, Nellie, recalled the gas radio's conception in a letter to *The Recorder*. Milnes's intensive experiments, she declared, 'achieved results beyond anything any scientist had ever done, though many had tried to develop a thermo-electric generator (and considerable sums had been expended by the Gaslight and Coke Company, who acknowledged that my husband had progressed far beyond anything they had achieved)'.

In the 1980s a former member of Milnes's staff recalled his employer as 'one of those pipe-smoking gentlemen who work through the night': in other words, the archetypal inventor of fiction. As a boy, he had converted a treacle-tin into a working steam engine, which subsequently exploded and hit the ceiling.

Milnes eventually became disheartened by what he considered bureaucratic interference with his business, and, in the 1950s, emigrated to New Zealand, where he died some twenty years later.

❉ ❉ ❉

CLASS

For a sweepstake race at York's renowned Knavesmire course in May 1791, certain rules were laid down. Each mount must carry twelve stones in weight and each jockey must be a gentleman. A horse named Centaur, ridden by a jockey named 'Kitty' Rowntree, was an easy winner. Rowntree was not a normal rider. He was seventy years old, one-eyed, and accoutred in dirty leather breeches and an ancient wig 'not worth eightpence', according to a hostile witness in a subsequent court case. The case arose from the refusal of the Clerk of the Course, one Robert Rhodes, who held the stake money, to hand over the winner's prize of £123 to Thomas Burdon, the horse's owner. The reason? Rowntree was not a gentleman.

Refusing to accept this ruling, Burdon took his complaint to court. The hearing was at York Guildhall a mere three months after the contentious race. Local landowners queued up to explain how they defined a gentleman and whether Rowntree fitted these definitions. No one disputed his honourable character, but the first witness, Sir William Foulis, who lived near Rowntree, denied he was a gentleman 'in the general acceptation of the word.' Burdon's senior counsel, a barrister fortuitously named Law, then asked if Rowntree enjoyed field sports and killed game 'like any other gentleman'. Sir William admitted that Rowntree had, in fact, been hunting before he (Sir William) was born. 'Did you ever know him do a dirty action?' asked Law. 'I never did,' conceded Sir William.

The next witness was John Preston, a farming friend of Rowntree, who confirmed strongly that he considered the old fellow a gentleman. Rowntree, who had his own smallholding, went to the markets just like other farmers. But when cross-examined for the defence, Preston admitted that Rowntree dined in a common eating-house so basic that few meals cost more than a shilling.

James Rule, a witness of the weighing-in, churlishly said that Rowntree might be a gentleman but he did not look much like one, while a sweepstake subscriber told the jury that Burdon himself was beyond the pale, never mind Rowntree, and that he had had cause to object to Burdon's own riding. Before the race, he had asked Rowntree how he could make such a fool of himself at his age. Rowntree had replied that he was sorry he came, that he did not pretend to be a gentleman, that, while in his cups, he had promised to ride Burdon's horse, and that 'he would sooner go home dead than break his word.'

Seizing on this last phrase, Law made a murmured but telling comment: 'Surely this is a little symptomatic of a gentleman. He seems to be the very pink of gentility.'

One of the other jockeys said he had told the Clerk of the Course that he would not ride with Rowntree. Asked if he had, in fact, ridden against 'Kitty', the jockey made the curious reply: 'I took no notice of him at all, but rode with the other gentlemen.'

Class distinctions of the time insisted that keeping hounds was gentlemanly, whereas having dogs that just mooched around was not. With this in mind, one of Rowntree's neighbours, who was also a Jockey Club member, was asked if the elderly person kept hounds. 'Certainly not!' he replied, confirming his contention that neither Rowntree nor Burdon was a gentleman. Another sweepstake subscriber said that any course in the land would object to Rowntree as a jockey: 'I have rode in similar sweepstakes for several, for the Prince of Wales, and I am certain if Rowntree had attempted to ride on such occasions he would have been kicked off the course.'

The last witness for the defence claimed that Rowntree kept hounds 'no more than I do a pack of archibishops'.

In his summing up, Law pointed out that no one had, in fact, come up with a real definition of a gentleman. Rowntree's dress and eating habits had been criticised, but what criteria were these? Rowntree, he said, had a small estate, enjoyed field sports, took out a licence to kill game and helped other gentlemen in preserving it from poachers:

> He follows no other occupation or business but pleasure, and if to be idle and useless is one of the prominent features of a gentleman, he has most fully in this instance proved his claim to that distinction. But when to these requisites I add the nicest sense of honour, the strictest adherence to a promise, that exquisite sensibility which is prepared to meet public insult, as well as private inconvenience, rather than break a promise made in a moment of partial inebriety, I think his character, on such a view of it, must stand high in the estimation of every man of honour.

At this the cheers that echoed through the court were so loud that the Lord Mayor went out to order candles so that the culprits might be identified.

Messrs Law, Burdon and Rowntree won the day, the jury finding for the plaintiffs, and the aged jockey went to his grave happy in the knowledge that he was a true gent. The law had said so.

PERKY PATRIARCHS

Yorkshire has had more than its fair share of doughty centenarians. Among them was Jenny Milner who lived in a thatched cottage in Baildon and was so respected that a narrow road was named Jenny Lane (still there) after her. In her old age she experienced hard times and, to make ends meet, made and sold besoms to housewives in the village and beyond. Her death in 1844 was widely mourned.

A rare book entitled *Yorkshire Longevity*, published in 1864, lists such characters as Valentine Cateby of Preston, near Hull, who died nearly two centuries ago aged 116. For the last twenty years of his life he ate nothing but biscuits and milk.

Simeon Ellerton of Crayke, near Easingwold, who died at 104 at the end of the eighteenth century, had the habit of walking the 150 miles to London on errands 'which he executed with singular fidelity and despatch'. A sturdy fellow all his life, he lived in a neat stone cottage he built himself, often carrying a suitable stone on his head for up to fifty miles.

Almost as tough was the widow Jane Garbutt of Welbury, near Northallerton, who died in 1865 aged 110. Her advice to those seeking to emulate her was probably: 'Sit up straight!' She invariably sat upright in her chair, rarely resting against its back. She also enjoyed smoking her pipe to the last, declaring that she had 'burned the fragrant weed' for nigh on a century.

Nearly all the ancient persons catalogued seem to have been active to the end. Jonathan Hartop of Aldborough, near Boroughbridge, died in 1791 at 138, still a revered cribbage player, 'keeping his own account, with the most perfect recollection of numbers'. He had five wives, the third said to be Oliver Cromwell's illegitimate daughter, and 140 great-great-grandchildren. He drank only milk and knew John Milton very well, once lending the hard-up poet £50 (though it would be irresponsible to suggest that this led to the writing of *Paradise Regained*).

The oldest Yorkshireman of all was Henry Jenkins, born in the little village of Ellerton-upon-Swale, near Catterick, in 1500 and living to be 169. He could well have been the oldest man in the world, said the anthology compiler, since the days of the Hebrew patriarchs. In his youth he toiled as a labourer. Later he became butler to Lord Conyer of Hornby Castle. Asked some time in the seventeenth century to name a public event he could remember, he referred to the 1513 Battle of Flodden, when, as a boy, he was 'sent to Northallerton with a horse-load of arrows', to be despatched to the English army. In his old age he was often summoned to give court evidence about ancient rights and usages, saving all concerned the boring chore of thumbing through yellowing law-books.

Hard work was Sarah Miller's recipe for old age. She was 103 when, in 1820, she was buried at Pateley Bridge, having hand-washed locally mined lead ore daily until she was 100. Time, she considered, was not to be wasted on any account. Thus she could be seen plying her knitting needles as she walked to and from work. Guests at her hundredth birthday party included several master miners who tucked into her goose pies with evident satisfaction.

Christopher Pivett of York did not make his century. He was a mere ninety-three when he died in 1796. But no fool he. After his home was burned down, he swore this was the last time he would be made to look an idiot. Never again, he resolved, would he sleep in a bed and leave himself little time to pick up his belongings in the event of another blaze. Thus for forty years he spent every night stretched, fully-clothed, across a couple of chairs or on the floor.

The smuggest of centenarians was Thomas Rollinson of Halton, Leeds, who died six years before Victoria ascended the throne. He had never been known to sing, whistle, swear or drink.

On the other hand, George Kirton of Oxnop Hall, near Reeth, who died aged 125 in 1764, 'was a remarkable instance that length of days are not always entailed on a life of temperance and sobriety, for no man – even till within a short time of his death – made more free with his bottle'.

Most intriguing of all is the case history of William Darnborough, for forty years sexton at Hartwith Chapel, near

Ripley. Before his death at 100 in 1846 he often related how, in his youth, he had watched the fairies dancing by moonlight on the moors. It was a matter of great regret to him that many had disappeared towards the end of his life, suggesting that there were times when extreme old age had its drawbacks.

✳ ✳ ✳

THE WILD WEST

In the 1880s people in West Yorkshire's Holme Valley played a somewhat indecorous game called Ringing Adam's Bells. It took place at the homes of those who lived in the region's scattered hamlets. Evenings of song and dance by the dim light of tallow candles became increasingly boisterous as strong ale, carried by children in long cans from the village inn, was supped. Eventually the children were locked out of the house, while the grown-ups indulged in their secret game. One small boy managed to peep through a hole in a paper window-blind and saw men and women seated facing each other in two circles on the floor, the men in the inner rings, the ladies in the outer. A fiddler in the centre played a lively tune as the women sang

> *Ring in th'owd Adam Bells*
> *Kitlins [kittens] i' t'clough.*
> *Who can see my bare arse?*

whereupon the women all fell backwards and threw their skirts over their heads while the men finished the verse with the line: 'Me, fair enough!' What followed had best be left to the imagination. Some forty years earlier a more respectable version of the game was played in public at wedding celebrations by women only. Adam Bells could have been a less-than-subtle reference to th'Owd Adam.

The citizens of the Holme and Colne Valleys were notably rough, probably because, cut off from the main communication routes, they were isolated from what might be termed civilizing influences. Many visitors were shocked by the fierce and brutal behaviour of the natives, who, in their turn, were suspicious of strangers and resistant to change. The travelling evangelist John Wesley wrote on 9 June, 1757: 'I rode over the mountains to Huddersfield. A wilder people I never saw in England. The men, women and children filled the streets and seemed just ready to devour us.' Two years later nothing had changed: 'Preached at Huddersfield to the wildest congregation I have seen in Yorkshire.' A Methodist preacher from Birstall wrote of preaching in the hills above Huddersfield 'where the people in general are little better than heathens, ignorant and wicked to a degree'. The men of Honley were so often drunk and violent they were nicknamed 'bulldogs'. They stoned strangers, practised bull-baiting and organised dog- and cock-fights.

In 1805, a vigilante group had been set up in Honley to combat the local drunkenness and disorder. Forty years later a *Leeds Mercury* writer was pleading for a mechanics' institute at Honley, describing the working-classes there as debauched, the drunks causing excessive damage at night.

When, in 1858, Queen Victoria was due to visit Leeds to ceremonially open the new town hall, a resident of the village of Holme penned a long poem that constituted an invitation to the monarch to make a diversion and drop by, despite the reputation of the place. It began:

> Most gracious, lovely Sovereign Queen,
> Unequalled in renown,
> E all yor routes, yun nivver been
> To visit us at Hown.

> But, as yur baan ta cum so near,
> Yu mud as weel cum nar,
> An see us reight, yun nout ta fear,
> As awkwud as we are.

> We han some oddish ways, for sure
> Un raither strange opinions,
> But ta ther Queen ther's nub'dy truer
> E all yur great dominions.

Yum tak no noatis what they sen,
Ut maks us into nout,
But cum an' have a peep, an' then
Yul nivver rue yur route.

The invitation was wisely ignored.

ALL ALONE

Between 1963 and 1969 the only active member of the Zion Baptist Chapel in Hebden Bridge was Florence Walton, born at the end of the nineteenth century. During that time she worshipped generally alone, as the only other church member was too ill to attend. She always left the door open, in case anyone else might wish to join her, but, apart from the occasional visiting minister from Haworth, she prayed alone. One Sunday she had been reading from Jeremiah a paragraph whose main point was that nothing was too hard for the Lord. When a visiting minister from the south of England arrived to conduct a service for her on that very day and preached from the same text, she felt the message was too strong to ignore and had the chapel redecorated so as to be fit for the Lord. Shortly afterwards, inspired by another Old Testament story, she had the chapel wired for electricity. In subsequent years, its membership increased.

THE LADY WITH THE EAR-TRUMPET

When twenty-year-old Constance Lascelles, a daughter of the fourth Earl of Harewood, married the third Lord Wenlock, she left behind the super-elegance of Harewood House in Leeds for the Hall in the Escrick Park estate outside York. This plain 'stucco box' she considered did not stand comparison with her former residence. As soon as she arrived, she asked: 'Where are all the griffins and sphinxes?' She was, however, a totally unstuffy woman, who was to preside over the Hall's social life for the last thirty years of Queen Victoria's reign and up to the beginning of the First World War, and was a passionate skater well into her seventies. Con-Con, as her family called her, surprised them by going out in London with a cashmere shawl around her shoulders, but no gloves or hat, which were deemed *de rigueur* for women in high society. Back home, she was kind enough to provide sanctuary for an over-imaginative niece who could not bear to stay in the London of Jack the Ripper. Younger visitors would climb a flight of red stairs pausing only to stroke the head of a huge tiger-skin on the landing (one of Wenlock's trophies from a visit to India). A compulsive amateur artist, Con-Con could usually be seen at her easel in the drawing-room, sometimes absorbed in the creation of landscapes of palms and tropical seas and featuring a tall figure in Oriental dress. She often rose before dawn to sit on a camp-stool and paint the sunrise, unperturbed about missing breakfast. She even designed wrought iron gates for the Hall's entrance. In her endeavours she received active encouragement from such eminent artists as Edward Burne-Jones, whom some considered one of the greatest English painters of the time.

A small, delicate woman with disconcertingly blue eyes, Con-Con was unfortunately absent-minded. When she lost a pen, she looked for it under 'P' in a French dictionary. To ensure that she should not confuse her guests' identities, she had them assembled before a meal in an ante-room, insisting they enter the dining room in strict order according to rank. She did not employ maids unless they attended church regularly, but was kindness itself to local villagers, presenting them with huge pots of cut flowers and loads of coal, and, for Christmas, logs and haunches of venison. She insisted they use the Hall's grounds 'as if they were your own'.

She became involved with an élite group called The Souls – well-born, intellectual and beautiful people, who ignored such traditional society pursuits as debutantes' balls, hunting, shooting and fishing, proclaimed the importance of art, the mind and personal relationships, and met at country house parties. They included the Tory statesman Arthur Balfour, Indian viceroy Lord Curzon and Margot Tennant, who became the second wife of Liberal statesman Herbert Asquith. They engaged in high-minded conversation and, in some cases, a little discreet adultery.

Over the years Con-Con became increasingly deaf and invested in several ear-trumpets, including one of silver for special occasions, and another of aluminium for everyday use. When, as often happened, she mislaid them, the entire household would be mobilised to search for them. One trumpet was so curiously shaped that fellow guests at a London ball mistook it for an ash-tray. The Prince of Wales escorted Con-Con into the dining room, and, when he spoke to her, she politely inclined her trumpet towards him. He was showered with cigarette butts. On another occasion, when she proffered her trumpet to an Italian duke who was her dinner companion, it was promptly filled with green peas.

LITIGIOUS LADY

Lady Anne Clifford was born at Skipton Castle in 1590. Her father died when she was fifteen, and first her mother and then Anne herself fought continuous legal battles to obtain her rightful inheritance. It was not, however, until she was fifty-three that the large family estates in the north reverted to her under the terms of her father's will. She was rightly respected for the restoration work she carried out, and was perpetually insistent on her legal rights, no matter what was at issue. One dispute concerned ownership of a hen she claimed was hers. To prove her point in court cost her the then enormous sum of £200, but when the case ended in her favour, she reputedly invited her opponent to a banquet at which the hen was the first main dish.

Despite Lady Anne's wealth and high social rank, she boasted she had never tasted wine. She did not need drink to loosen her tongue, and the poet John Donne, one of her house guests, observed that she could discuss anything from predestination to silk, knowledge of the latter bolstered by her childhood hobby of keeping silkworms.

In her old age she was invited to take a trip to London and the glamorous royal court. If she were ever tempted to make such a journey, this true northern lady replied, she would need to wear a horse's blinkers to avoid seeing anything that might offend her. Increasingly idiosyncratic, she regularly cut her finger-and toe-nails then carefully burned the parings to prevent them being used in witchcraft ceremonies.

❉ ❉ ❉

THE SECOND JULIUS CAESAR

When the artist Julius Caesar Ibbetson had completed a painting, he would stick it in his window, then stand back and lend an ear to the comments of passing youngsters. Children, he opined, were honest and never stooped to unworthy flattery.

Ibbetson was born in 1759 at Farnley Moor, near Leeds. He was named Julius after a grandfather, and Caesar because of his birth by Caesarean section, an operation his mother did not survive. At twelve he was apprenticed to a Hull painter of ships and showed an aptitude for the elaborate decorations captains of the day liked for their prows and sterns. Four years later he attracted the attention of a Yorkshire theatre manager and comedian, for whom he began painting stage sets. At seventeen he ran away to London, where he quickly made his name as a journeyman artist, specialising in scenes in royal parks. He was twenty-six when he had his first picture hung at the Royal Academy. It showed Thames shipping and countryside. From then until 1815 hardly a year passed when he did not exhibit at the RA. His most exotic venture was a trip to Java, where he bowed to a local king who spoke no English and said: 'My dear fellow, I don't know about your titles, but I must say I never saw such an ugly fellow in my life – never. Do get shaved and look like a Christian.' His expression was so solemn that his speech was applauded.

At forty-five, he brought his family to Masham, where he painted prolifically for most of what proved to be the last twelve years of his life. He developed a dislike of the exploitation of artists by art dealers he considered philistines. These so-called arbiters of taste, he railed, 'live luxuriously out of works of art; for which they feel the same affection as a butcher does for a fat ox'.

He became part of Masham's social scene and doubled his work rate there, producing landscapes and portraits of both the local élite and more proletarian characters. National figures, including royalty, joined the subscription list for a book of his etchings. He also assumed parochial responsibilities, becoming a trustee of the Masham – Thirsk road. He caught a cold while painting the favourite hunting horse of the Duke of Cleveland's daughter, and died at fifty-eight. His Masham churchyard epitaph describes him as 'eminent for his taste and skill in painting rustic figures, cattle and rural scenes'.

He may also have been rather cunning. A story is told of a publican who asked him to paint a lion on his inn sign. Ibbetson asked if he wanted the lion chained. 'No,' said the landlord. 'It would hardly run away.' After Ibbetson had painted the beast in watercolours it did just that: disappearing as soon as it rained. When the innkeeper relented and said he would like a chained lion after all, Ibbetson re-made the painting in oils.

CLICK-CLICK-CLICK

From the seventeenth to the nineteenth century, men, women and children in the Dales were incessant knitters. Nowhere more so than in the town of Dent. Here people knitted as they sat in their chairs, stood in their doorways and strolled along the country lanes. There was no stopping them. The poet Robert Southey dubbed them The Terrible Knitters of Dent ('terrible' being dialect for 'great') and the name stuck. Many of them depended on their obsession to earn enough cash to buy the little extras that made life comfortable.

Husband and wife knitting outside their Dales home

(Courtesy of Marie Hartley and Joan Ingilby)

They knitted stockings, gloves, jackets and nightcaps, ferried across the Cumbrian border to Kendal in covered carts. On winter evenings they gathered round a neighbour's blazing fire and knitted with a speed that reportedly 'cheated the eye'. In *The Rural Life of England* (1844), William Howitt reported: 'They sit rocking to and fro like so many weird wizards. They burn no candle, but knit by the light of the peat fire.' As they knitted, they gossiped and sang, and the tune of a hymn, 'Dentsdale' (No. 804 in the Methodist Hymn Book), was based on an original knitting song. Their implements were crooked sticks called pricks, which were said to produce rhythmic music as they clicked, and, when not in use, were stored in a wooden holster, as large as a dagger's sheath, attached to a belt called a cowband. Girls often received cowbands as gifts from their sweethearts.

According to Howitt, the women knitted after completing their household chores. They did so 'as they walk about their garden, or go from one village to another'. Old men who sat knitting round the fire pinned cloth around their shins to prevent them being scorched: '. . . sometimes they may be seen on a bench at the house front, and where they have come out to cool themselves, sitting in a row knitting with their shin-cloths on, making the oddest appearance imaginable.' People knitted on their way to church, and one local parson began a service by ordering his congregation to lay down their knitting sticks as they were about to pray.

Neighbouring Garsdale was the eighteenth-century birthplace

of John Dawson, a farmer's son, who by day tended sheep in a field but at night knitted stockings like all his playmates. Allowed to spend his 'knitting brass' as he chose, he bought the books that set him on his career as Dr Dawson, eminent mathematician. Navvies building railway lines for the track from Settle to Carlisle were also taught how to knit in their spare time.

❉ ❉ ❉

THE YORKSHIRE PYGMIES

Colonel James Harrison was a landowner whose redbrick mansion, Brandesburton Hall, near Beverley, was surrounded by a hundred-acre park, to which Harrison invited several cricketing celebrities to play his own scratch eleven. His main reputation, however, was as an explorer. In 1885 he made his first trip (to South America), and over the next three decades he travelled extensively in Africa and the Far East, largely to hunt big game, which he brought home and had scientifically catalogued to aid academic studies. He eventually owned 1,300 stuffed animals and birds, keeping a staff of taxidermists constantly employed and working on the preservation of many specimens himself. Every room overflowed with his hunting trophies, elephant tusks adorning the fireplace and a hippo's head on the billiard-room mantelpiece. The Hall was virtually a museum, containing what may have been the world's largest collection of animal trophies, examined by natural historians from all over Europe.

He was most attracted to what was then the Belgian Congo. Penetrating the heart of the country's Ituri Forest, he was conducted to a village occupied by a little-known pygmy tribe. When they attacked a government deputation, killing seventeen of them, he remained unperturbed and quickly gained the pygmies' confidence: to such an extent that six of them – four men and two women – agreed to accompany him back to England. Aged between eighteen and thirty-four, and ranging in height from 3ft 8ins to 4ft 6ins, they were named Bokane (the chief), Kuarke,

Mongona, Mafutiminga, Matuka and Amuriape. Permission having been granted by the Belgian government, they were issued with clothing, and left Africa with the colonel in May 1905. The following month they made their London debut, photographed on the House of Commons terrace flanked by a group of august personages. At dinners laid on for them, they sat at table with their arrows never out of reach, and bows hung around their necks.

Col. James Harrison (fourth from left) on the House of Commons terrace with the pygmies he brought to Yorkshire.
(Courtesy of *Country Life*)

From London, Harrison took the pygmies to Brandesburton, where he gave them the complete freedom of his extensive woodland, and, to the locals' amazement, they lost no time in building their own brushwood kraal (a village of huts) in the lush parkland, and fashioning spears in a nearby smithy. The park's tall trees gave them the opportunity to enjoy rope-climbing, and they demonstrated their various skills to the many visitors who came to see them, and who, on Sunday afternoons, observed their bizarre attempts to cope with knives and forks, not to mention the strange foods.

The pygmies astonished onlookers by eating not only the honey from Harrison's hives but the bees. They also dined on sparrows they had shot, and became adept at hunting rabbits. When a local youth made himself a nuisance, they chased him off in a hail of arrows. Despite such skirmishes, their forbidding appearance to European eyes, and their warlike disposition, they were reportedly even-tempered and easily amused. For the medical experts who examined them they provided much previously unknown information about the human species.

Harrison meanwhile was cultivating personal friendships with the Prince of Wales and the American president, Theodore Roosevelt, who shared the colonel's devotion to rugged, outdoor activities. He also entertained Indian princes. But much of his time was occupied with the pygmies, whom he exhibited in many towns, often in music-halls. They appeared in Hull, where he erected an African village to illustrate his plan to improve conditions among pygmy tribes. During an exhibition of the pygmies at the London Hippodrome, he met his wife-to-be, a rich American singer, whose family had pioneered the manufacture of Stetson hats. Harrison took his bride back to Brandesburton, where her car became a new curiosity.

In 1904 Harrison was consulted by King Leopold of the Belgians about atrocities allegedly committed against Congo natives, and many subsequent reforms were based on the colonel's suggestions.

It is not clear why, after two years, the pygmies eventually left Yorkshire. The rumours were that they could no longer abide the cold weather or that they had fallen victims to pneumonia. Their departure may merely have indicated that they had lost their curiosity value. In any event, they sailed from Hull in the autumn of 1907 and returned to the Ituri forest, where Harrison visited them twice. His death at sixty-five in 1923 was the indirect result of an old wound incurred when he was savagely mauled by a lion.

Before he died he had donated much of his valuable collection to Scarborough's Wood End Museum. During a painstaking re-cataloguing of the museum's possessions in 2000, a safe was opened. Inside was a stuffed pygmy antelope, a rare animal. The museum authorities hoped that, nearly eighty years after Harrison's death, it could not only aid research into the species but help it achieve protected-breed status.

❄ ❄ ❄

PORNO POLITICO

If he had been alive today Richard Monckton Milnes, later ennobled as Lord Houghton, would have been gleefully exposed by the Sunday tabloids. Milnes was MP for Pontefract, a Tory who eventually switched to the Liberals, simultaneously resigning his membership of the élite Carlton Club, which he dismissed as a 'political scullery'. He was a biographer of John Keats and was himself a minor poet of some distinction. He lived in Fryston Hall, a gaunt, pillared mansion near pleasant woodland five miles from his constituency. Its library was his favourite place of relaxation. Here he kept the treasured autographs of famous hangmen (though opposing the public executions of the time) and a series of books about school punishments. But most remarkable were the shelves lined with indiscreet material, mostly in the form of eighteenth century French and Italian novels secretly smuggled into Britain. These included all the available printed works, along with manuscript fragments, of the notorious Marquis de Sade, who Milnes conceded was 'odiously famous'. Among those who shared his tastes, he called his house Aphrodisiopolis. On Sunday mornings, if his guests were easily shockable, he had, it was reported, the impish habit of showing them the choicest exotica in his library before they set off with his wife for church. He also found it intensely amusing to watch guests recoil when he held out for inspection a piece of the dried skin of a notorious murderer, which he kept, like a crushed flower, between the pages of a book. In a letter written to the painter Dante Gabriel Rossetti, the poet Algernon Swinburne referred to Milnes glowingly: 'His erotic collection of books, engravings etc is unrivalled upon earth – unequalled, I should imagine, in heaven. Nothing low, nothing that is not good and genuine in the way of art and literature is admitted. There is every edition of every work of our dear and honoured (sic) Marquis.'

To many, at this time, the very idea of a novel in French, let alone the horrors of de Sade, was anathema. On one occasion the statesman-historian Sir George Trevelyan ordered young Swinburne (virtually a protégé of Milnes) out of the house after the poet had loaned Lady Trevelyan a volume of Balzac's *La Comédie Humaine*. Trevelyan then cast the book on the fire, an incident that Swinburne presumably related with relish on one of his visits to Fryston Hall.

In view of the general attitude towards publications of a salacious nature, Milnes had to resort to devious methods to get his hands on them. One book for which he had searched for a long time in vain was finally bought for him by a contact in Paris and sent to England with the pages gummed together in case it was picked up by a nosey Customs official. The contact was probably his regular supplier, Fred Hankey, a notorious, yellow-haired ex-Guardsman described by one acquaintance as 'a second de Sade without the intellect'. Hankey slipped small books into the overcoat pockets of a relative's valet. Others he sealed in the bag of a sympathetic Queen's Messenger returning from Constantinople with despatches for the statesman Lord Palmerston. He also sent books to Milnes in the British Embassy bag, addressed to a friend of Hankey's in the Foreign Office. Milnes' favourite courier was a Mr Harris, manager of London's Covent Garden Theatre, who conveniently made frequent professional trips to France 'on musical business'.

Milnes had a long friendship with Sir Richard Burton, the explorer and expert on the erotic literature and practices of the Arab world. Burton made several visits to Fryston Hall, and Milnes wrote a favourable review of one of Burton's books, while

*The last portrait of
Lord Houghton,
(Richard Monckton Milnes)
painted two years before his death
by Rudolf Lehmann*

using political connections to get Burton to destinations he wished to investigate. Less sympathetic towards Milnes was a learned professor who, in one of his books, described the MP as a man of 'Mephistophelean malice', who had guided poor Swinburne 'through the Inferno of his library', a man of the world crouching like a spider and deriving evil pleasure from watching his guests' interactions with each other. Milnes used his friends 'as instruments in order to put together some strange rural comedy'. Likewise, Benjamin Disraeli found Milnes vain, envious and trivial. To the prime minister's wife Lady Russell, Milnes was, in a word, gross, while the first secretary at the American Embassy called him 'smutty'. In fact, Milnes was a bluff character and an excellent conversationalist, though he did hold an extravagantly high opinion of himself. In a commonplace book he wrote: 'Oh, how wide is the diapason of my mind! From what a height to what a depth!' After Milnes' death, even Swinburne, while describing his patron as 'a good-natured old fellow', said that when he became a peer, his title might well have been Baron Tattle of Scandal.

Milnes never lacked for distinguished guests. The Palmerstons were frequent visitors. A young American attaché who paid 'a wonderful visit' said his host was perhaps the sanest among those present 'in spite of his superficial eccentricity, for Yorkshire sanity was true to a standard of his own, if not to other conventions'. Alfred Lord Tennyson stayed at Fryston Hall during an unfortunate period when it was in a state of disrepair. Ceilings had collapsed, and rooms were damp and rickety. The great poet called the house

Freezetown. William Makepeace Thackeray, who was wined and dined there for a week, seems to have been luckier. 'Fryston,' he said, 'combines the freedom of the tavern with the elegance of the château.'

With symbolical appropriateness, a large part of Yorkshire's hottest library was destroyed, along with the house, by a fire (cause unknown) in 1876, while Milnes himself was in Dublin. Of the local firemen's attempts to quell the blaze he was somewhat churlish. 'The loss,' he said, 'would have been hundreds [of pounds], not thousands, had the Pomfret engine been effective, but it would not work, and the hose was as rotten as the ancient borough.' The house was rebuilt, but in 1932 was eventually demolished, its portico, with an irony Milnes would have appreciated, going into the construction of a new Baptist church in Airedale.

By the time Richard Monckton Milnes, Lord Houghton, died, he had lived at Fryston fifty years, a Yorkshire landowner who, oddly, hated the land and country pursuits. His passing was mourned by one of the indigent poets he had helped in the following lines:

Adieu, dear Yorkshire Milnes! we think not now
Of coronet or laurel on thy brow;
The kindest, faithfullest of friends wast thou.

MAGIC MEN

Thomas Denton was a Yorkshireman who started life as a tin-smith, but, through a love of literature, went on to run a York bookshop. His interests diversified when, in 1784, he saw a Speaking Figure exhibited by an ingenious Frenchman. It took the form of a doll, suspended by cords or ribbons, that answered questions. He made a copy of the novelty and exhibited it around the country, before selling it to a printer. He now turned his hand to the manufacture of mathematical and scientific instruments, including pantographs (instruments for copying drawings and plans), a Writing Figure, various other automata, and a 'celestial bed' that guaranteed fertility to childless couples who slept in it. Denton made a fatal error when he linked up with John Jones, a well-known coiner. They were arrested and both, on conviction, were sentenced to death: in Denton's case for the possession of coining implements. He and Jones, it was reported, 'died professed infidels'. From his death cell Denton had written a letter to his parents:

> Hon. father and mother. When you receive this, I shall be gone to the country from whence no traveller returns. Don't cast any reflection on my wife; she has been the best of wives, the best of mothers, and the best of women; and if ever woman went to heaven, she will. If I had taken her advice, I should not have been in this situation . . . The bell is tolling. Adieu.

Buried near the altar steps in St Gregory's Church, Bedale, is another dabbler in esoteric arts, Gustavus Katterfelto, quack, charlatan and early pioneer of the art of conjuring. The son of a Prussian army officer, he descended on Britain in 1781 to entertain audiences with his smoke-and-mirrors performances, incidentally describing himself as England's greatest philosopher since Isaac Newton. One of his stage assistants was a black cat to which he attributed extraordinary talents. His notoriety stems from his rôle as a peddler of dubious, five-shilling nostrums during a flu epidemic. He got what some saw as his comeuppance when a hot-air balloon he had built landed on a hayrick and set it on fire. Not having the cash to compensate the Yorkshire farmer who owned the rick, he was thrown in jail. He often visited Whitby, where audiences applauded one of his most popular tricks: raising his daughter to the ceiling with a huge magnet after she had donned a massive steel helmet held in place by leather straps under her armpits. At Whitby he collected fossils, ammonites and agates which he displayed in a travelling exhibition.

When Katterfelto's popularity waned, he was barely able to eke out an existence, and was imprisoned again, this time as a vagrant and impostor. He died at a Bedale Inn in 1799. *The Gentleman's Magazine* carried a simple notice: 'At Bedale, co.

York, the eccentric Dr Katterfelto, whose advertisements of himself and his black cat used generally to be ushered in with the word "Wonders!" three times repeated.' His Whitby links were maintained after his death when his widow married one of the town's publicans, John Carter, later instrumental in the revival of the local jet industry.

※ ※ ※

THE SHOELESS SQUIRE

In 2000 a new gallery at the Wakefield Museum was named after and dedicated to Charles Waterton, the locally born, nineteenth-century naturalist. The family home had, for three centuries, been Walton Hall nearby, and its parkland was ideal for anyone fascinated by animal life. Waterton's interests were quickly recognised at school, where he was appointed the establishment's official rat-catcher, fox-taker and polecat-killer. After leaving school he fell victim to a lung condition and was sent to Demerara, in British Guyana, to recover. There he managed family estates and took part in an expedition into the jungle to acquire samples of curare, the native Indians' arrow poison, then thought to be a possible cure for tetanus. For his journey he chose the rainy season, but travelled barefoot, because, he explained, socks and shoes would have slowed his progress when chasing beasts. Convinced of the value of blood-letting (which he called 'tapping the claret'), he became intrigued by the local vampire bats, expressing indignation when they refused to attack his big toe when he left it protruding from his hammock as he slept. After almost dying from malaria, he returned to Demerara, where he was nursed back to health, and the reports of his jungle jaunt made him such a celebrity that a ball was held in his honour.

He returned to Yorkshire to take up his position as Squire of Walton Hall, where he transformed its 260-acre park into a bird sanctuary. Here he allowed nothing to be killed except the brown rat, which he regarded as a Continental intruder and the enemy of the nearly extinct, native black rat, which he called 'the poor injured Briton'.

In 1817, his wanderlust resurfacing, he went to Rome, where he climbed to the top of St Peter's to leave his gloves in the lightning conductor. The Pope reportedly appealed for volunteers to remove them. When none came forward, Waterton himself retrieved them. Three years later he returned to British Guyana, where he dealt with a giant boa constrictor by tying its jaws together with his braces. Having set his heart on adding a big cayman, or alligator, to his creature collection, he barbed and baited sticks which he attached to a rope tied round a tree. When a cayman was hooked he leapt on its back and seized its forelegs. Asked later how he had managed to keep his seat, he put it down to the years he had spent hunting in England.

Back home, Waterton returned to the seclusion of Walton Hall, round which he built a giant wall. Eventually, however, he began to suffer from his old complaint, itchy feet. He sailed to the USA, to study the bird life, he said. When he sprained his foot alighting from a stage-coach, he plunged it beneath the waters of Niagara Falls.

Returning yet again to Demerara, he made a creature of his own from the skin of a red howler monkey, manipulating the features into the resemblance of a human face. He called it his 'Non-descript', an engraving of which appeared as the frontispiece to his *Wanderings,* published in 1825. Some people assumed it was a caricature of a Treasury official with whom he had once crossed swords, but Waterton insisted it represented no one in particular.

The Non-Descript

When Waterton married, he and his bride spent their honeymoon touring museums. Less than a year later, his wife died giving birth to his son. He now spent much of his time in a sparsely furnished room at the top of the house, creating a chapel alongside it. Most of each day he passed reading or working in the grounds. When twenty-eight rattlesnakes were used during a Leeds experiment to test the value of curare, Waterton made an appearance to grab and hold the reptiles as they bit rabbits. Invited to Regent's Park Zoo in London, he expressed concern at the doleful features of a fierce orang-utan, and insisted on stepping into its cage, where the two embraced with apparent affection. He also had friendly encounters with a cheetah and a chimpanzee.

When he made annual Christmas visits to his old Lancashire school, Stonyhurst, he would often wear bizarre disguises or make his appearance walking on all fours.

Despite his eccentricity, he was a kindly man. He often allowed the public into part of his park, which he converted into a recreation area with swings for the children and picnic spots for their parents. Every year mental hospital patients would visit the park, and Waterton would spend the whole day in their company, rowing them round the lake and dancing with them. If he met a barefoot beggar he would hand the unfortunate fellow a knife he carried for this specific purpose and urge him to take it to the cobbler's to exchange for a pair of boots. He celebrated his eighty-second birthday by kicking off his own shoes to shin up an oak. He caught his foot in a bramble, fell heavily against a log, and two days later died.

DRINK UP

Claimed, in some quarters, to be part of man's vital spirit, it is, in the ordinary course of events, discharged in the privacy of one's bathroom, the process being delicately described as spending a penny or washing one's hands. Once the job is done, there's an end of it. But in Yorkshire this was not always the case. In the mills, workers would scour wool with it, and collectors would often stroll past the looms with buckets soliciting contributions. Charity schools in eighteenth-century Cleveland boasted small troughs in which the fluid was stored for later use by clothworkers. The liquid was also used to bleach aprons, remove stains and wash clothes and blankets. With bare feet, housewives would trample on clothes in tubs of the liquid before rinsing them all in a stream.

An eighteenth-century poem gives an account of (literally) oily mill workers who each morning would soak themselves in a vat of the fermenting liquid compounded with pig-dung. Soap, at the time, was a relatively expensive luxury, and even when the price was reduced, people found the liquid much gentler than soap's hard alkali. The stuff, it has also been claimed, was great for getting rid of machine grease and had an astringency that discouraged blackheads. Addicts also swore by it as a hand lotion, and a Brighouse woman told an interviewer of watching her mother, a midwife, remove a baby's nappy and promptly wipe his face with it to give him 'a lovely skin.' Even shampoos containing the fluid were popular, especially for dealing with greasy hair, and the liquid's acid content may also have loosened dandruff. The typical Yorkshire housewife kept a special receptacle for storing the all-purpose fluid, which she used, with hot water, to scrub floors. Combined with bracken ashes, it proved handy for putting a sheen on pewter. People also used the liquid to bathe chapped hands, styes and bleary, morning-after eyes. Many swore blind that it would remove warts and that a good remedy for chilblains was to stick one's toes in a chamber-pot. Current expert opinion is that this is hogwash, there being no evidence that such practices would have worked, and application of the liquid would, indeed, have caused a stinging sensation that distracted attention from the underlying pain. The fluid was also used cosmetically. In Honley, a few years ago, an elderly woman recalled how her grandmother would wash in it before kissing her wincing children. To be fair, the lady's face was surprisingly wrinkle-free.

The liquid was even drunk. In the 1920s, in Honley, a herbalist, Norman Brookes, would urge customers to sup their own personal fluid every morning for health purposes. One client said years later that the drink was tolerable after one became accustomed to the bitter, salty taste. More sceptical was the husband of an enthusiast who had downed gallons of the stuff over the years. 'If thi body's thrown it aat once,' he opined, 'ah can't see that it's baan ter do much for a second time araand.' Scientists, apparently, share this view.

❉ ❉ ❉

PROPHETESS

Mother Shipton was the British equivalent of Nostradamus. You would not have missed her, even in a crowd. She had 'large bones, staring eyes and mis-shaped legs'. Her best feature, however, was her nose, which was 'of an incredible and unproportional length, having in it many crooks and turnings, adorned with strange pimples of diverse colours . . . which . . . gave such lustre in the dead of night that her nurse needed no other light to assist her in the performance of her duties'. This possibly refers to the attendant at her birth, which allegedly occurred in a Knaresborough cave during a thunderstorm in 1488. Oddly, no published mention of her dating before 1641 has ever been found. In that year an anonymous pamphlet appeared, bearing her likeness on the title page, and claiming that Cardinal Wolsey, on his nomination as Archbishop of York, was annoyed to hear that Mother Shipton had predicted he would never even enter that city. He was so irked that he sent three friends to threaten her with punishment unless she retracted her prophecy. Undaunted by the appearance of these heavies on her doorstep, she stood firm, wined and dined them, and made forecasts about their own fortunes, not to mention many startling events that would shake the kingdom and certainly her own locality. Some of her predictions have been taken as foretelling the Civil Wars. As for Wolsey, he was preparing to leave for York, when he was arrested for high treason, was imprisoned in the Tower of London, and never did enter York.

The old lady spawned a host of copyists, and her meteorological predictions multiplied at an alarming rate. People in all walks of society agreed she was an exceptional seer, and the diarist Samuel Pepys related that when Prince Rupert heard, while sailing along the Thames on 20 October, 1666, of the outbreak of the Fire of London, he drily commented, 'Now Shipton's prophecy is out.' A seventeenth-century author, Richard Head, best known as the writer of the fake autobiography of a professional thief, leapt on the Shipton bandwagon, publishing what purported to be a full account of the talented lady's life, and unkindly representing her as the Devil's daughter. Her hideous, witch-like appearance and power of prophesying disasters (of which he invented several instances) proved her paternity, he reasoned. Head's book went into several reprints, and was further developed in the anonymous *Strange and Wonderful History of Mother Shipton*, which recorded that she was born Ursula Southiel, married a carpenter named Toby Shipton when she was twenty-four, and, after enjoying a wide reputation as a necromancer, died at seventy-three. Over the years, innumerable chapbooks were printed, most in the North of England, repeating her prophecies in various forms.

In 1862 an entrepreneur named Charles Hindley printed a garbled version of Head's work, adding verses foretelling the inventions of the steam-engine, the electric telegraph ('around the world thoughts shall fly in the twinkling of an eye') and the end of the world in 1881. Before the world was scheduled to implode, however, Hindley confessed that his opus was a forgery.

Mother Shipton.

Spurious memorials to Mother Shipton appeared in various locations. A sculptured stone said to mark her grave near York proved to be the mutilated effigy of a knight in armour, probably filched from his tomb. Another stone reported to mark Mother Shipton's last resting place turned out to be a copy of a Roman tablet. An imaginative engraving of Ma Shipton in a chariot drawn, as if she were Santa Claus, by a reindeer, appeared in the well-named *Wonderful Magazine* in 1793. The so-called Mother Shipton moth derives its name from the resemblance of its wing markings to the profile of an old woman with hooked nose and upturned chin.

Mother Shipton's prophecies are almost too numerous to mention. They foretold the coming of the motor-car, the dissolution of Knaresborough Priory, the building of a house of glass (the Crystal Palace, of course), the destruction of a York bridge in a flood, the Gunpowder Plot, the coming of iron ships and of aeroplanes, and the day when men would walk on the sea-bed. She has been immortalised by that hallowed record of notable English figures of the past, the Dictionary of National Biography. Yet it is quite possible that not only her amazing talent but she herself was the figment of others' imagination. If you find this distressing, you can always drown your misery in Knaresborough's best-known pub. It is called the Mother Shipton Inn.

CHAPTER 2

LITERARY LINKS

TWO MEN IN A SUIT

One of the most thrusting of Victorian entrepreneurs, Samson Fox was a Leeds mill-worker's son, starting work in the same mill at the age of eight. At fifteen he was an iron foundry apprentice. Years later he set up the Leeds Forge Company, achieving international publicity during the Zulu War when the world's first steamer to be fitted with a boiler of his own invention sailed to South Africa in record time. He marked his success by moving home from Leeds to rather more upmarket Harrogate. When Queen Victoria's grandson, Prince Albert Victor, visited the spa town to open the Royal Bath Hospital, rebuilt largely through Fox's munificence, the businessman paid for the construction of two ornamental arches over Albert's route. They were embellished with royal heraldic devices and crowned by a replica of Fox's boiler. Another clever Fox invention was a pressed-steel railway bogie, for the American marketing of which he hired Diamond Jim Brady, the American ex-bellhop who became a flamboyant financier.

Samson listed music among his recreations, creating at the Leeds Forge what was then adjudged the world's finest brass band. A meeting with American operatic soprano Lilian Nordica encouraged him to present the Prince of Wales with a £45,000 cheque towards the building of the Royal College of Music. When the Prince formally opened the College, it was Fox who handed him the golden key that did the job.

But trouble was brewing at the Forge. In 1889 Fox formed the so-called Water Gas Syndicate, to promote the use of gas produced in a novel fashion, by blowing steam through beds of red-hot coke. The end result, he insisted, was cheaper than conventional gaslight and, furthermore, didn't smoke. To demonstrate his point, he built Europe's first water-gas street-lighting plant in the centre of Harrogate, attracting visitors from all over the North who came to goggle at one of the wonders of the age. The syndicate, however, went bust, ruining many investors. The news reached the ears of Jerome K. Jerome, whose *Three Men In A Boat*, coincidentally, had been published the year the syndicate was set up. Already co-founder of *The Idler*, a successful monthly magazine, he was now running *To-day*, a twopenny weekly with a tough editorial policy. But none of his journal's literary outbursts was to cause as much trouble as an article by his city editor accusing Fox of a deliberate scam. Fox sued for libel, explaining that he had been accused of inducing the public to subscribe the capital of the Leeds Forge Company and several water-gas companies, fleecing them of £46,000 and funding the Royal College of Music to give a wrong impression of his commercial prosperity.

Heard in the Queen's Bench Division of the High Court, the case was long (thirty days), complex (even Jerome, with little business background, did not seem to know what it was all about) and essentially boring. A galaxy of legal talent had been assembled: four silks for Fox and three for Jerome. The writer felt confident the case would be thrown out after a brief hearing. Fox won, but was awarded damages of one farthing. Both men were ordered to pay their own costs: £11,000 in Fox's case, £9,000 from Jerome.

When it was all over, Fox, a short, round Pickwickian figure, met Jerome in a court corridor, where the two shook hands. Fox told Jerome: 'I'm going back to Leeds to strangle my solicitors. I hope you'll do likewise.' For Jerome the case was a financial disaster, but the resilient Fox survived. His court-house handshake suggests he had forgiven the writer. But had he? A few years later, he became a Parliamentary candidate. His chosen constituency? Walsall, Jerome's native town. Fox, however, did not live to fight the election, dying at sixty-five of blood poisoning after a tour of the United States and Canada.

THE RIPON WONDERLAND

Alice Liddell, daughter of lexicographer Henry George Liddell, was the little girl for whom Lewis Carroll wrote *Alice's Adventures in Wonderland*. Charles Dodgson (the author's real name) had been Liddell's colleague at Oxford, being a respected mathematics lecturer, and thus knew the family well. But before the book was published, Carroll had another child in mind: Mary Hilton Badcock of Ripon.

Carroll was strolling through Ripon, when in the window of a photographer's studio, he saw a portrait of Mary, daughter of the principal of the then new Ripon College. He sent a copy to his illustrator Sir John Tenniel, asking him to use Mary as his model for Alice. Tenniel testily replied that he no more needed a model than Carroll needed multiplication tables. Nonetheless, it is thought the artist may have visited Mary to make preliminary sketches. Certainly Carroll sent her a first edition of *Alice Through The Looking-Glass* inscribed, 'from the Author, Christmas, 1871'.

There was even a Ripon link with Alice Liddell. As a boy, her father had spent a wretched four years as a pupil in the city's Bishopton Grove School (subsequently a guest-house).

Carroll was twenty when his father, archdeacon of Richmond and rector of Croft, on the Yorkshire–Durham border, was also appointed canon of the recently established Ripon Cathedral. This meant that father and son had to live in Ripon thirteen weeks in the year, and there seems little doubt that the Cathedral inspired Carroll's more fantastic creations. He would have seen carvings of a griffin chasing a rabbit, a mermaid with hairbrush and mirror, creatures (known as Blemmyes) with eyes and mouths in their breasts, brawling dragons, a pelican feeding her young, two pigs dancing to bagpipes played by a third, and a bench-end elephant floating on a turtle's back. He would also have been familiar with a passage leading to the crypt, and this may have inspired the rabbit-hole down which Alice tumbled into a magical new world. (Also worth mentioning in this connection are the gypsum deposits with which Ripon is pocked and which are notorious for the sudden appearance of discommoding craters.) When the architect Sir George Gilbert Scott carried out a major restoration of the Cathedral, he introduced, high in the south transept, a Queen of Hearts, sword in hand, against a red background, and a Cheshire Cat, as obeisance to Carroll.

One Ripon family Carroll visited was that of the Revd Hugh Cunningham, chaplain to the local House of Correction. One of Cunningham's daughters, Maggie, filched a glove belonging to Carroll (whether accidentally or with malice aforethought is not known). For this Carroll sent her 'a little bill', an incident recognisable in *Alice in Wonderland*.

In 2000, some 400 members of the Lewis Carroll Society flocked to Ripon to absorb the atmosphere of the city that played a part in the creation of Carroll's great works.

❇ ❇ ❇

BY JINGO!

A Bradford clergyman's son educated at Bradford Grammar School, Charles Hyne created a once-popular fictional character, Captain Kettle, who first appeared in 1898 and survived forty years. Himself a seasoned sailor, Hyne based Kettle on a ship's master whom he encountered in the Gulf of Mexico and who kept his crew in order with a pistol. A chauvinist who despised all things non-British, Kettle would be hastily removed from library shelves today.

❇ ❇ ❇

MR STOKER'S NIGHTMARE

At a seafood shop in Whitby the author Bram Stoker had rather too many helpings of dressed crabs. These (his son later reported) gave him the nightmares that inspired his *Dracula*, one of the world's most notorious books.

It was during a three-week holiday in Whitby in August, 1890, that Stoker began taking notes for the novel. He had arrived from London after what must have been an excruciating eight-hour train journey with his wife Florence and their eleven-year-old son Noel. They booked rooms with a sea view, and Stoker enjoyed long walks by the shore and along the cliff paths, mixing with the locals and listening to their yarns about shipwrecks and superstitions. He showed interest in dialect and recorded the tombstone epitaphs of drowned sailors. During his research in a Pier Road library (now a restaurant), he came across the name Dracula in *An Account of the Principalities of Wallachia and Moldavia* by one William Wilkinson, who revealed that the Wallachian word Dracula meant Devil. From the local coastguard and the *Whitby Gazette*, Stoker learned about a Russian brigantine, the *Dmitry*, from the port of Narva, that ran aground here in 1885. In the novel Count Dracula leaps off the *Demeter*, a Russian ship from Varna, in the shape of a dog. The churchyard where Dracula claimed his first victim remains much as Stoker described it. One of Stoker's biographers also described a low gravestone with fossilised skull and crossbones, that might, he said, have inspired the novelist's reference to a master mariner 'murdered by pirates off the coast of the Andes'. In the book, the passing of a cloud reveals first the ruins of Whitby Abbey and then 'a half-reclining figure, snowy white', in the moonlight. Then something is observed over the figure.

Whitby has never forgotten its Dracula link and has introduced visitors to various vampiric experiences. Actors disguised as Dracula have lurked around street corners to spring on unwary passers-by, and one high-tech innovation has been an animatronic Dracula. There are raffles to raise funds for the welfare of bats and an annual Dracula ball for which frightening dress is preferred.

The town also boasts a Dracula Trail, starting at the Victorian-style Bram Stoker Memorial Seat at the south end of Spion Kop, with a setting carefully chosen to give the visitor the same view the dyspeptic author had when he was plotting his novel. The Trail includes East Crescent, in one of whose small houses the story's

Wreck of The Dmitry of Narva on Whitby sands: inspiration for a crucial episode in Bram Stoker's Dracula.
Photograph by Frank Meadow Sutcliffe. The Sutcliffe Gallery, Whitby

(Courtesy of Whitby Literary and Philosophical Society)

heroine Mina and her friend Lucy are spending the summer holidays; the railway station, where Count Dracula leaves Whitby for London in one of his fifty boxes; and of course the 199 stone steps of the famous Church Stairs, up which Mina rushes in a frantic dash to rescue Lucy. People on the Trail can also see Henrietta Street, linked with the thost-dog (a variant of Yorkshire's Barghest), a dog-like goblin portending death, once believed to haunt Haggerlythe, as the street was once called.

CHRISTIAN SOLDIERS AND WEREWOLVES

On a hot spring day in 1864, a tall handsome man stepped off the train that steamed into the station at Horbury, near Wakefield. Despite the weather, he wore a frock coat and walked with some difficulty under the weight of what looked like a sleeping-bag draped over his shoulders and hanging down to the ground. Boys at a school at which he had recently taught had called it a Black Slug. It was, in fact, a travelling bag he had devised himself and had carried on travels in Iceland, where he had strapped it to a luckless pony's back.

The man was Horbury's new curate, Sabine Baring-Gould, who, as he reached the first houses, heard the approach of a band playing 'See The Conquering Hero Comes'. Looking back, he saw a procession of men walking two-by-two in their Sunday best. Leaving the Slug in a shop, he joined the parade and asked one of the men who was being honoured by this stirring event. 'Don't know,' was the reply. 'T'aint me.' The band stopped at a pub for refreshments, then marched on. Baring-Gould eventually learned this was part of the annual gala of the local non-denominational school. He made off as quickly as possible to the vicarage.

For a man at the start of a new career, Horbury, whose inhabitants were canal boatmen or in the shoddy or coal-mining trades, was not exactly ideal. Its streams steamed with effluent and the workers into whom Baring-Gould was expected to instil reverence for matters divine were a rough lot, whose pastimes included organising cock-fights, playing knur and spell (a very old form of tip-cat), racing pigeons, coursing rabbits with whippets, drinking prodigiously and betting on almost anything you could think of. They were certainly not addicted to religious devotions.

As Baring-Gould walked, during his first days, along the muddy streets, groups of shawled, suspicious women would fall silent, though eventually they came to regard him as a good man. Years later, he was to portray the local characters in two novels, *The Pennycomequicks* and *Through Flood and Shame*. There is a veritable gallery of them in his *Yorkshire Oddities*, including a butcher who took his wife to Bolton for a week's honeymoon, and, on their return, put her on the scales, divided the wedding expenses by her weight, and frowned: 'Lass, thou'st cost me fourteen pence a pound. That's the dearest bit o' meat I iver bought.'

Baring-Gould rented a small cottage, whose ground floor he opened as a night school. His voluntary helpers included a former monk who now hawked muffins. His chucker-out was a woolcomber who, at the sight of potential trouble-makers, would crush two walnuts in his fist and roar: 'If you don't take care, I'll crack your heads as I do these 'ere.'

The new curate quickly became known for his fertile imagination, and boys and girls refused to leave the cottage until he had told them a story. He formed a choir, and when boys pelted his windows with mud or hurled old boots at those walking to his services, he would rush out the back door, grab the ringleader, drag him into the house and take the first steps involved in transforming him into a choir-boy. Initially his choristers sucked toffees or peeled oranges during practice. They soon learned this was not acceptable behaviour.

One day Baring-Gould spent ten minutes or so 'knocking off' the words of a hymn for the children to march to over a hill for the Whit Sunday festival service. At first he set it to a tune he arranged from the slow movement of Haydn's Symphony in D. When this proved unsatisfactory, he replaced it with a Sir Arthur Sullivan melody. The hymn was to comfort Queen Victoria in her old age and achieve international renown, though some objected to what they called its militaristic overtones. It was called *Onward Christian Soldiers*.

Baring-Gould fell in love with Grace Taylor, a local girl in clogs who had worked in the mill since the age of ten, when her first job was tying up bundles of worsted. Their happy marriage was to last forty-seven years.

Two years after his arrival in Horbury, Baring-Gould was appointed vicar of Dalton, then an obscure hamlet of a hundred souls near Rotherham. It was popularly known as Dalton i't Muck, and he found it somewhat less congenial than Horbury.

Among his tribulations was the bossiness of the local aristocrat, Viscountess Downe, daughter of a Bishop of Bath and Wells, who kept an eagle eye on a clock near her pew to make sure his sermons did not overrun their allotted time. If he should sin in this respect, the lady expressed her displeasure by depriving him of the wines and fruits she normally sent down from the big house.

It could have been the gloom in Dalton that persuaded Baring-Gould to spend part of his time there writing a book about were-wolves. Altogether he was to pen a hundred literary works: histories, biographies, reminiscences, novels, fairy tales and ghost stories. Despite the importance he attached to education, he lamented the fact that, as the peasantry became more knowledgeable, they ceased to believe in fairies and pixies.

❆ ❆ ❆

THE MYSTERIOUS AFFAIR AT
THE OLD SWAN

In 2000 the Crime Writers' Association held their annual meeting in Harrogate's Old Swan Hotel. The choice of venue was deliberate and singularly appropriate. For it was here that one of the most famous mystery writers of the twentieth century, Agatha Christie, was discovered after an eleven-day disappearance that baffled and intrigued the nation.

In happened in 1926 when Agatha was living with her husband, Colonel Archie Christie, a First World War flying ace, and their six-year-old daughter Rosalind at Styles, a country house in Sunningdale, Berkshire. The colonel had a mistress, Nancy Neele, eleven years younger than Agatha, whom he wished to marry. On 3 December Archie left to spend the weekend with Nancy at the home of friends in Guildford, Surrey. They were later to admit that the weekend was planned as 'an unofficial engagement party'. It was probably Archie's projected trip that sparked a row, partly overheard by a maid, between the colonel and the author. When

Archie eventually left, Agatha tucked up her daughter and petted the family terrier as usual.

Early the next day her Morris Cowley car was found abandoned with its headlights on, near the edge of a chalk pit at the foot of a grass slope, fourteen miles from her home and six from the colonel's weekend rendezvous. In the car was Agatha's fur coat and a suitcase containing more of her clothes. At Styles there was no sign of her.

Police fruitlessly combed the area, including a pond called Silent Pool. They also escorted Colonel Christie back home. They failed, however, to spot him picking up a note from his wife, which he never disclosed, presumably because it contained embarrassing references to his behaviour. But it could not have explained her disappearance. If it had, the colonel would have used it to dispel police suspicions that he had murdered her. Agatha's secretary, Charlotte Fisher, knew of the note, but agreed to the colonel's request not to mention it. In a second note, to Charlotte, passed to the police, Agatha wrote: 'My head is bursting. I cannot stay in the house.' The note asked Charlotte to cancel a hotel booking in Beverley, where she had been planning to spend the weekend. Mailed in London on the morning she vanished, another letter, to her brother-in-law at his business address, said she intended to spend the weekend at an unnamed Yorkshire spa.

Attention immediately focused on Harrogate, but when the registrars of hotels checked by police yielded no trace of the writer's name, this line of inquiry was unforgivably dropped.

Among those drawn into the mystery was Sir Arthur Conan Doyle, creator of Sherlock Holmes and dabbler in sprirituism. Somehow he obtained one of Agatha's gloves and handed it to a medium (who had presumably been reading the papers). The medium announced: 'There is trouble connected with this article. The person who owns it is half-dazed and half-purposeful. Her name is Agatha and she is alive. You will hear of her next Wednesday.' He was only a day out in his prediction.

On 12 December two members of the dance band at Harrogate's Hydro Hotel (now The Old Swan) told police that a woman who might be Agatha Christie was staying in the hotel. In a plain knitted dress she had danced to the tune of *Yes, We Have No Bananas* in the ballroom. To check the story, police entered the woman's room, where they found a picture of Agatha's daughter. They summoned her husband.

The climax came as Agatha descended the hotel stairs for dinner, now in a stylish evening gown. Positioned behind a newspaper he was pretending to read, the colonel signalled to the police, who confronted her. Seconds later her husband joined them. 'Shall we go in for dinner?' he asked his wife. This they did, eating a quiet meal at a corner table.

It later emerged that Agatha, hoping to shock her husband, had managed the entire affair with the skill she normally devoted to creating one of her intricate plots. She had let her car roll down the slope to the chalk pit and had left her clothes inside the vehicle to add to the mystery. She had expected to be discovered in two or three days at the most.

After dancing at the hotel, she had occupied her time knitting, making up a bridge foursome, writing and playing billiards. She claimed she had lost her memory, a story that did not hold water as she had confided all the details of her scheme to a friend at whose London home she had spent the weekend after abandoning her car. She had even bought special clothes for the great adventure.

The episode hastened the end of Agatha's marriage. Within weeks Styles was up for sale and the couple soon divorced. Agatha's friends were divided about her behaviour. She split them into FODs (members of the Faithful Order of Dogs) and FORs (Faithless Order of Rats). One of the latter was presumably the actor, composer and radio presenter Hubert Gregg, with whom Agatha worked on the direction of five plays. He recently claimed that her disappearance was no more than a publicity stunt. The book she wrote after her Harrogate escapade was *The Mystery of the Blue Train*, dedicated to 'two distinguished members of the FOD'. First editions are particularly prized.

One of many other literary celebrities who had visited Harrogate was Charles Dickens, who gave public readings in the

Spa Rooms and said the town was 'the queerest place with the strangest people in it, leading the oddest lives of dancing, newspaper reading, and tables-d'hôte'. He sounds like a prophet.

CHAPTER 3

ODD SPOTS

LOST BUT NOT FORGOTTEN

Until half a century ago little or nothing was known about how most medieval folk lived. Most histories of the period concentrated on the documents of lords and masters, the peasants considered scarcely worth serious scholastic study. Such lowly persons were regarded as unknowns, the evidence of their lives permanently lost. Despite this appalling lack of knowledge, several assumptions were made about medieval rural life, among them the notion that village life was relentlessly grim for peasants, who lived in wretched hovels with barely enough to eat. Another belief was that rural England's basic geography – networks of villages encircled by open fields – had remained more or less fixed since early Anglo-Saxon times.

It was not until 1952 that understanding of this period was transformed by excavation work that began in a lost Yorkshire Wolds village called Wharram Percy. At that time Wharram, virtually ignored by scholars, was little more than a field of lumps and bumps surrounding a decaying church in a remote valley. One man, however, realised that it was potentially an archaeological (if metaphorical) gold-mine. Maurice Beresford had already begun pioneering work on medieval landscape remains, identifying deserted villages and fields in the Midlands. Now he came to Wharram, to start a gargantuan research project that was to last forty years and revolutionise medieval and landscape archaeology. Wharram saw the first excavation of a medieval peasant house, the first complete excavation of a parish church and the first recovery of a large medieval population from a cemetery. The diggings proved that, far from inhabiting hovels, the peasants of Wharram lived in long, spacious, well-built houses. Moreover, these were kept meticulously clean, the floors swept so often they were now almost concave. So sophisticated were these homes that they boasted windows, furniture and door-locks and latches. Beresford's team also discovered several items of dress adornment such as bronze buckles and straps, not to mention many coins. It became clear that the richer peasants had lots of money to take to market to buy domestic goods.

The village apparently died in the earth sixteenth century. By that time, house floors, previously wood, were of stone. The houses were substantial enough to have stood for two centuries or more. One complete surprise was the finding of an abandoned twelfth century manor house beneath a row of peasant homes. Some homes were linked together, while a new type of courtyard farm was built alongside older longhouses, suggesting that media-eval villages were constantly changing. Beresford's examination of the church showed that side aisles had been built to accommodate newly fashioned and privately endowed altars. Wharram's human remains made up one of the largest collections of skeletons experts had been given the opportunity to study. Many subsequent findings were hardly surprising: fractures not always well set and tooth decay common, for instance. More intriguingly, the level of left-handedness proved to be, at sixteen per cent, twice the modern world average, suggesting there was no social pressure favouring the right hand. A 1997 study indicated that the peasants of Wharram may have eaten as much fish as the citizens of York, implying more regular contact with the outside world than one would have expected.

Another lost community is in the region of what was once known as Ravenser, whose story was first investigated in the nineteenth century. Diggings around the present Spurn Point unearthed stone, chiselled and laid in lime, apparently the foundation of a building of some note in its day. Ravenser was indeed an important town, first mentioned in an eleventh century Icelandic poem. Tradition has it that it was from Ravenser that invading Norwegians, defeated by the Saxons under King Harold at Stamford Bridge, near York, in 1066, finally sailed off in ignominy. In the thirteenth century an accretion of gravel, perhaps around a ship-wreck, developed off-shore into an island large enough for a vessel to run aground on it. The hulk remained there until it became the home of an enterprising tradesman who sold provisions to the crews of passing ships. The Lord of Holderness, William de Fortibus, thought the island sufficiently lucrative to be taken over for his own profit, and sent over a bailiff and colleagues to found a hamlet there on his behalf. This became Ravenser Odd, or Ravensrod, which fishermen found convenient as a spot on which to dry their nets as well as stock up with food.

This new town grew and prospered, King Henry III giving it the right to hold a weekly market and an annual sixteen-day fair, which proved to be another draw for shipowners. During this time most of the inhabitants of the old Ravenser left for the new community, while local monks acquired a share in Ravenser Odd's profits and were allowed to erect buildings in which to kipper herrings.

The townsfolk of Ravenser Odd were dedicated entrepreneurs. They hailed ships to offer higher prices for their fish catches than they could get at Grimsby, their original destination. Complaints to Edward I brought the seething merchants of Grimsby no redress, and insult was added to injury when both Hull and Ravenser Odd were granted the privileged status of 'free ports' on payment of £300 to the king. By the end of his reign, Ravenser Odd was even represented in Parliament.

Less than a century after the island had created itself, however, the ominous signs of its fate were appearing. All along the Humber unpredictable tides had been wreaking coastal havoc. In 1301 a funeral cortège carrying a body from Hull chapel to Hessle for burial was washed away by a flood tide. Travelling between Hull and Anlaby (today a city suburb) had become so risky that the road had to be raised six feet.

The end of Ravenser Odd was as dramatic as its première appearance. In the 1340s the waves of the Humber destroyed a chapel and the greater part of the town, after which it was largely abandoned. The final disaster came when, according to a chronicle of the period, the waves had 'risen above the town and surrounded the place like a solid wall'. The few survivors roamed the town carrying relics of the saints, a cross and ecclesiastical ornaments in a last-ditch attempt to invoke divine intervention. Eventually the town was totally abandoned, the refugees dispersing to a variety of destinations. In 1355 a great storm devastated one of Ravenser Odd's main burial grounds, washing away many bodies. An abbot was directed to collect the remains and give them Christian burial elsewhere. By the end of the fourteenth century, the island had been transformed into a mudbank. Over the centuries the onslaught of the elements has left the old Ravenser to revert to nature.

IRRITATING

In the 1970s, as part of a modernisation scheme at Elland Road, the Leeds United ground, the Scratching Shed was demolished. This was the literally irritating name of a stand originally built on a steep bank, so that spectators resembled people on a hillside. They were so uncomfortable they would kick the earth about until they had improvised little platforms that enabled them to keep their feet flat on the ground. This shuffling – or scratching – around gave the stand its name.

THE BAG OF BONES

The hamlet of Kirkdale, near Pickering, is the location of the strange story of the Yorkshire hyenas. The first event in this tale was the decision by John Gibson, an Essex manufacturing chemist, to spend a holiday in his native Yorkshire. Visiting friends, he happened to pass through Kirkdale, where, beside a road under repair by workmen, he noticed a large pile of stones and bones. When he inquired about them, he was told they came from a limestone quarry near by. Quarrymen, it turned out, had uncovered, in a steep rock-face, the mouth of a dank and gloomy cave that housed a remarkable scattering of animal bones, many cemented together by stalagmites. Attaching little importance to the discovery, they assumed the bones to be the remains of dead cattle. But the astute Gibson quickly realised they were the bones of no known British animals. As news of the find spread, scholastic curio-hunters descended on Kirkdale, collected specimens and took them home. Recalling the scene later, the Revd William Eastmead, a member of the Yorkshire, Hull and Whitby Literary and Philosophical Societies, described men of science crawling, by torchlight, on all fours through the 'particularly grotesque' cave. Other visitors, wrote Eastmead, included literary men dressed as rustics, with handkerchiefs wrapped round their heads, and their faces and hands patched with mud. Soon there were bones galore in the display cabinets of drawing-rooms in Scarborough, Whitby, Bridlington, Hull and York. A Kirkbymoorside cleric commandeered an elephant's thigh-bone. Sir George Cayley, the squire of Brompton, near Northallerton, shipped a heavy bag of bones to an eminent expert on extinct animals who lived in Paris. Other sample relics reached Professor William Buckland, an eccentric Oxford don.

Buckland was fond of riding round the country on an old black mare, carrying with him a geological hammer and a blue specimen bag. In December, Buckland travelled with his bag to Kirkdale, where he found a long and narrow cave, some four feet square for most of the 100 yards or so that had been penetrated. The floor was covered with mud. The cart-load of bones he found were mostly broken into tiny fragments. Many were crumbling. Some, which appeared to have been gnawed, projected from the mud 'like the legs of pigeons through a pie-crust'. Buckland then compiled an extraordinary 'visitors' book' listing all the animals that, from the evidence, had once entered the cave. These included up to 300 hyenas, and much smaller numbers of tigers, elephants, bears, wolves, foxes, rhinoceroses, hippopotamuses, bison and various birds and small creatures.

Buckland then proclaimed his amazing conclusion. The sediment of mud, he said, had been left by the onslaught of the Biblical Flood. The hyenas, he explained, had inhabited the cave before the Flood. The other creatures were their victims, carried there from other parts of the world by the raging and universal waters of the deluge, and then slaughtered and eaten, no doubt to the accompaniment of the most ghastly laughter ever heard. Buckland's thesis was seized on by theologians and clerics who had long been fighting to prove what they believed to be the literal truth of the Bible story. During a lecture on his findings, Buckland suddenly stopped, turned to a famous judge sitting in the audience, and said: 'And now, my lord, what do you think of that?' The judge promptly replied: 'Such facts, brought as evidence against a man, would be quite sufficient to convict and even hang him.' Satirical friends of Buckland penned verses describing the demise of 'The Last English Hyena' as it was overwhelmed by the encroaching Flood:

> *But ere it rose to mix him with the rest,*
> *Thus did he growl aloud his last bequest:*
> *'My skull to William Buckland I bequeath',*
> *He moaned – and ocean's wave he sank beneath.*

When Buckland himself wrote a book about his discoveries with the forbidding title *Reliquiae Diluvianae* (Relics of the Flood), it became a best-seller and went into a second printing. The Royal Society, the nation's most distinguished scientific body, awarded him a medal. The Geological Society elected him their president. Others, however, treated his conclusions with derision. A magazine called *The Sphinx* sneered at 'the idea of authenticating a divine revelation by the bones of tom-tits, hyenas and water-rats.' A *Gentleman's Magazine* correspondent drily attributed Buckland's views to 'the gift of second sight', and proposed that, pending further visions, a bazaar should be opened for the sale of bones, sand, gravel and other relics of the Flood.

Some twenty years later Buckland recanted, admitting that his reference to the Flood had been a mistake, and that the mud in the cave had been glacial in origin. His erstwhile supporters were furious. When in 1844 the British Association for the Advancement of Science met in York, feelings ran high. The 'railway king', George Hudson, who was to preside at a dinner given by the corporation in honour of the delegates, arranged for the withdrawal of all invitations to geologists. 'We've decided,' he said, 'for Moses and the Dean' (of York who had gone on record as opposing Buckland's recantation). Buckland was, however, accorded many honours before he died in 1856. He eventually became Dean of Westminster. He was also popular at fashionable parties, to which he would often bring his famous blue bag.

❄ ❄ ❄

FAKES

If there are not enough ruins in your neighbourhood to attract historically inclined tourists, why not build your own? The idea has been taken up in various parts of Yorkshire. A monument known as Yorke's Folly, near Pately Bridge, for instance, dominates an extensive stretch of Nidderdale, and looks intriguingly under the weather. It is, however, a mock ruin, created some two centuries ago thanks to the generosity of John Yorke, a local landowner, who may have been influenced by pictures of similar structures near the Rhine. The workmen, who were delighted to do the job at a time of wide unemployment were paid in both hard cash and bread. Since then visitors have been under the pleasurable illusion that they are looking at the remains of an old monastery. Originally, it consisted of three columns, thus becoming known as Three Stoops, but in 1893 a fierce gale brought one pillar down, ironically creating a genuine ruinous effect. Another sham historical structure, St David's Ruin, near Bingley, looks like a medieval castle that has been shot to pieces. Consisting of a 'ruined' circular tower that has been likened to a giant chess piece, with an arch alongside, it was erected in 1796 by another ambitious and not particularly squeamish landowner. Ashe Hall, near Richmond, boasts a mock Gothic temple. It was put up by the Zetland family, who also erected a fortified tower known as Oliver's Ducket, said to have been modelled on a ruined outpost of Richmond Castle, formerly on the same site. ('Ducket' was a local name for 'dove-cote', an appropriate name in view of the openings for cannons that became nesting places for birds.) At Hunmanby there is a two-centuries-old mock medieval arch at the entrance to the grounds of Hunmanby Hall. The stone used in its construction came from the Brigg, the promontory jutting out into the North Sea at Filey. Mock fortifications form part of the walls protecting the estate of Castle Howard, Yorkshire's most renowned stately home. Dating from the eighteenth century, they remind the viewer that, until 1693, a castle did, in fact, stand on the site of the present mansion. Finally, near Masham in Wensleydale, there is a historic treasure that purports to be a Yorkshire version of Stonehenge: stone circles and standing pillars supporting crosspieces. A huge boulder resembling an enormous table is often taken to be all that remains of a Druids' temple. It was all built in the nineteenth-century by a local squire who thought it would be nice to look at.

MONSTROUS PIES

Denby Dale, near Huddersfield, is renowed as the village that marks momentous occasions by baking gargantuan meat and potato pies which are fed to the populace after being paraded through the streets. The first, in 1788, celebrated the mad King George III's return to sanity. The second, celebrating the victory at Waterloo, contained a mixture of mutton and fowl. The third, marking the 1846 Repeal of the Corn Laws, was paraded through the village on a wagon drawn by thirteen horses. But as the pie was about to be cut, disaster struck. The platform on which it stood collapsed, and the pie plopped to the ground, to be pounced on by 15,000 people jostling for the broken pieces. The tragedy was rumoured to have been engineered by Tories in an attempt to ruin the largely Liberal celebrations. Another theory is that it was a malicious attempt to cut short a long-winded speech by knocking out some of the platform supports. The fourth pie, marking Queen Victoria's golden jubilee in 1887, consisted of beef, veal, lamb, mutton, pork, pigeons, chickens, hares, rabbits, grouse, ducks, plovers, turkeys, geese, small birds, suet, potatoes, and a skinned fox. A professional London chef supervised the baking, but to no avail. Not surprisingly, the pie went a bit 'off', bystanders recoiled, and it had to be buried in quicklime in a nearby wood. Local housewives salvaged the village's reputation by producing their own Resurrection Pie, which was not quiet as large. The next pie marked the 1896 jubilee of the Repeal of the Corn Laws. Because of post-war austerity, no pie was baked to commemorate the end of the First World War, but that baked in 1928 – known as the Infirmary Pie because the money raised was to endow a Huddersfield Royal Infirmary bed – was considered a delayed celebration. The Coronation Pie was a flop. Wartime restrictions were still in force, and villagers applied to the Ministry of Food for a special allocation of meat and fat. This was turned down, and the celebrations went ahead without a pie, an offer of 1,400 pounds of beef from an Australian farmers' and settlers' association being politely declined. The 1964 pie marked the birth of four royal babies, not even conceived when the initial plans were made. Seventy thousand people ate the 1988 pie, which marked the event's 200th anniversary. In 2000, in keeping with the age, the makers of the Millennium Pie set up their own website and summoned the aid of specialist technology, Huddersfield University mechanical engineers being hired to test the design of the six-tonne pie-dish, constructed of twenty-four stainless steel containers enclosed in a cradle, to ensure it did not buckle and collapse under the strain. It all worked admirably and the 1846 fiasco was not repeated.

GOING DOWN

You cannot descend deeper into the bowels of the earth anywhere in Britain other than in Gaping Ghyll Hole at Ingleborough in the Yorkshire Dales. This fearful cavern is 110 metres deep, 137 metres long and 40 metres wide, and its main chamber can swallow York Minster. Pothole clubs occasionally help adventurous or reckless citizens to go down in a bosun's chair operated by a winch. The journey takes little more than a minute. Potholers have spread apocryphal stories about the winch braking at the last possible second after operators had been distracted by a passing walker's shapely legs. If true, it should not happen again, as electronics experts have now devised a black box which gives out digital pulses to calculate the depth, and bleeps loudly when it is time to stop the winch. Guided tours of the floodlit main chamber are available for non-cavers.

❄ ❄ ❄

HORSE ON A HILL

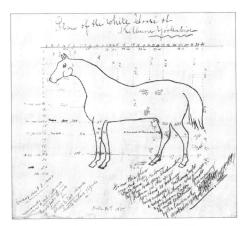

Original plan for The White Horse of Kilburn

One of the nation's great landmarks is the huge white horse cut on a hillside at Kilburn in 1857 by Jerry Hodgson, the village schoolmaster, and a team of dedicated helpers. Hodgson undertook the formidable job at the behest of Thomas Taylor, a local man who had made a fortune from cheese and bacon, and hoped the horse would perpetuate his memory.

65

Hodgson went to racing stables at Hambleton to sketch horses in training and used the drawings as the basis of a figure covering some two acres. It is 318 feet from nose to tail and 220 feet tall. Over the years since the figure was carved, it has needed several restorations, for which enormous quantities of limestone have proved helpful. In 2000 one of Hodgson's drawings fetched £2,400 at a Driffield auction. It had once been owned by a Kilburn policeman and previously came up for auction in 1976. Also in 2000, an artist who may have been slightly miffed by the horse's perpetual popularity, laid an outline of an elegant sofa, fashioned from strips of cloth, on a hillside overlooking Harewood House in Leeds. This, however, was only temporary.

❄ ❄ ❄

STREETWISE

Land of Green Ginger is the romantic name of a Hull city-centre street inhabited by a bank, solicitors and a couple of business-men's pubs. Investigating the name's origin is a pursuit destined to end in frustration or even migraines. Many explanations have caught the public fancy. One is that the area was part of the garden of one of Henry VIII's palaces that boasted a plot in which green ginger, a medieval court luxury, was cultivated. Another is that the name is a corruption of Lindegren Jonger (Lindegren the Younger), a Dutchman who lived in the neighbourhood. More simply, the name is said to be derived from the many warehouses here that stored the spices unloaded from ships in the harbour. Others believe the name derives from the spicy plants grown on an estate which was owned by a family of importers and of which the street marked a boundary. The earliest known reference to Land of Green Ginger is in a 1735 history of Hull.

An even more bizarrely named street is Whip-Ma-Whop-Ma-Gate in York. It is said to have once been the scene of public thrashings. Another tale is that Mass was being celebrated in a nearby church when a dog made off with a chunk of holy bread.

The congregation chased it out of the church, led by the priest. The pursuit ended in the street, where he cruelly urged the crowd to whip it without mercy.

❉ ❉ ❉

C'EST MAGNIFIQUE

On a visit to the Eiffel Tower you may find washing fluttering on a line in its front yard and cats snoozing beside its dustbin. Not that you are likely to be rubbing shoulders with hundreds of tourists. The Eiffel Tower in question is 30 feet tall and can speedily be reached by train from Leeds. It is a Gothic-style house, topped by a gloomy belfry, in Hebden Bridge. It is not called the Eiffel Tower through a passing whim, the name being engraved in stone within a blackened arch above the front door. The inscription also discloses that the building was completed in 1893, a mere four years after the original Eiffel Tower. The house, with its view of mill roofs in a mini-valley, stands on the corner of Eiffel Street and adjoins a four-storey row of flats called Eiffel Buildings. It all sounds like a self-deprecating joke.

❉ ❉ ❉

AS THE DRIVEN SNOW

Retired sergeant-majors around the country must have sobbed uncontrollably when, in the 1970s, a shabby Sheffield factory was closed and sold to a garage. It was here that the private soldier's bane, Blanco, had been made. Blanco was the preparation that replaced pipeclay as the universal substitute for whitening the webbing in a soldier's equipment. Its name came to symbolise hard, monotonous labour. It was invented in 1881 by John Pickering, whose Sheffield firm had hitherto specialised in assorted polishes. The firm's actual boss, John's father, Joseph Pickering, even found a place in a contemporary volume about England's leading personalities. The article lauded Blanco as being 'hailed with joy in military circles' since it greatly surpassed pipeclay 'in evenness of colour, uniformity and ease of application'. Squaddies surely sniggered at this encomium. Nonetheless, the stuff's reputation spread around the world, and, as a result, soldiers named White became generally known as Blanco White. One slang dictionary, however, felt it necessary to mention that the nickname had no connection with one Blanco White, a poet and theologian who died in 1841. The Pickerings remained Blanco's sole manufacturers until it finally faded out. Even when they ceased operations, they kept its formula secret.

❄ ❄ ❄

PETRIFIED

The Dropping Well in Knaresborough is a cascade of water falling into a rock pool (which also serves as a wishing well). Below water running over a projecting block of limestone visitors hang gloves, hats and eggs, which become encrusted with the lime, sulphates, chlorides and magnesia that the water contains. Within four months the objects appear to have been turned into brown stone. Attempts to crack the eggs are futile.

❄ ❄ ❄

THE BRIDGE BUILT FOR LOVE

It was at a fair that Tom Ferres, a Cleveland farm worker, danced and promptly fell in love with a fair-haired girl. When the dance was over, he led her to the refreshment tent, where he learned that she was Agnes, daughter of a wealthy Glaisdale farmer, Squire Richardson. When Ferres asked him for his daughter's hand, he scornfully replied that he would never allow her to marry 'a beggar'. Undaunted, Tom disclosed his ambition to go to sea, help despoil the Spanish Armada, and return with untold riches. Impressed, the squire said that even if Ferres had only tolerable success in such an exploit, he could wed the girl. Until then, he ordered, the couple must not see each other. They did, however, manage the occasional nocturnal rendezvous when Agnes would place a lighted candle in her window to signal the all-clear.

For these meetings Ferres had to cross the River Esk, using stepping-stones: a tricky business when the river was swollen. This inspired him to make a rash promise. If he returned from his naval adventures a wealthy man, he would build a crossing, to be known as Beggar's Bridge, for the benefit of future sweethearts and in memory of his own amour.

When an appeal went out for local volunteers to defend the country against a threatened Spanish invasion, Ferres seized the opportunity. He signed up as a crew member on a merchant ship, the *St Hilda*, on the way to Plymouth to seek out the Armada.

Storms had delayed the Spanish fleet, but as soon as they were sighted, they were subjected to continuous cannon-fire. Ferres himself helped launch fireships against the Armada, now anchored off Calais. With the enemy vanquished, the *St Hilda* was ordered to make for the Spanish colonies across the Atlantic. Ferres was appointed a buccaneer captain's lieutenant, becoming involved in a series of piratical exploits, plundering gold-laden galleons and capturing officers who were only released on payment of large ransoms.

The victors sailed back to England and entered Whitby harbour, where they were cheered by a huge crowd on the quayside. When the spoils were divided, Ferres found himself even richer than Squire Richardson, who received him with open arms and gave permission for the wedding. The ceremony was marked by a grand fête in Glaisdale.

Ferres became a Hull shipbuilder and kept his promise to construct Beggar's Bridge, now a prominent Esk Valley landmark.

SOME BARE FACTS

The façade of a building that overlooks Settle market-place boasts a carving of an unclothed male figure known as The Naked Man. Dated 1663, it recalls that the building was once the Naked Man Inn. How it got that name is not clear, though it could be a satirical allusion to Settle folk's lack of interest in their personal apparel. Such apathy was understandable as a toll of a halfpenny for every new hat worn on market days scarcely encouraged the wearing of chic attire. The Naked Man was covered up when Queen Victoria passed through the town, even though the date obscures the parts that might have offended her.

✻ ✻ ✻

HOT VELVET

In the year 1900 Harrogate council decided to take advantage of a growing demand for the odd practice of bathing in peat. It extended this facility into the Montpellier Pump Room (built in 1870 on a site that is now the Lounge Hall Car Park). The *Harrogate Advertiser* was ecstatic:

> It is an exceedingly comfortable bath, and is practically adapted for rheumatism, rheumatic gout, internal inflammation and some forms of skin diseases . . . The effect of the bath may be described as comparing it to a huge poultice . . . The peat mud, of which there is an abundant supply, will be brought from the corporation water works . . . and is of very fine quality. It will be specially prepared and free from all scratchy or objectionable particles. Once used, the peat will then be removed, a fresh supply being kept in the recess behind the building.

This lengthy encomium, however, was probably not half as effective as the brief but graphic testimonial of a reader who described the peat bath sensation as 'rather erotic – it felt as if your body was being enveloped with quantities of hot velvet'.

Harrogate's reputation as a spa town first spread around the country in the 1620s, when visitors raved about the alleged medicinal properties of the mineral springs in what was then a straggling agricultural village in the Forest of Knaresborough. The rheumaticky and the gouty flocked there to bathe in treated sulphur water and two new settlements grew up, one consisting of a group of lodging houses with adjoining bath-tubs to which the water was carted in casks.

In the off-season the entrepreneurial natives would boil gallons of sulphur water to extract Harrogate Salts, sold as far afield as London. One local source was nicknamed Tewit Well after the tewits (lapwings) that gathered there to feed on the mineral encrustations forming around the well head as the water evaporated. Tewit water was said to purge the blood of 'cholericke, phlegmaticke and melancholicke humours' and, as a sideline, cheer and revive the spirits, strengthen the stomach and improve the appetite and consequent digestion. Another spring won a reputation as a wash for sore eyes.

Most of the seekers after good health or hypochondriacs who came to Harrogate, which became known as the 'first English Spaw' (sic), were well-heeled. They were generally the only ones who could afford the trip, and they gave the town what might be called its tone, which it has conscientiously preserved. Their numbers increased when many new springs were discovered in the late eighteenth and early nineteenth centuries.

So famous did Harrogate eventually become for its waters that many people were convinced it lay beside the sea. When the comedian Dan Leno performed there in 1904, he reportedly inquired: 'Where are the sands?' and chances are he was not joking.

Between the two world wars, Harrogate slipped into a decline, partly because of the Depression, and partly through a change in medical opinion about the value of mineral waters. The domed Royal Pump Room, which was built in 1842 to enhance the Old Sulphur Well, and where, in August 1898 (a good year for statisticians) 31,546 glasses of water were served, was closed, later to become a museum, with displays of various spa treatments and an opportunity to sample the strong sulphur water. But one can still be stylishly pampered at the Royal Baths Assembly Rooms.

SPLIT PERSONALITY

The most mixed-up community in Yorkshire is Barnoldswick, whose county boundaries are a constant topic of heated debate. Though the town stands within Yorkshire's historic boundary, it was encircled in 1974 by new administrative borders lumping it with Lancashire for local government purposes. In recognition of this confusion, the town crier sports both white (for Yorkshire) and red (for Lancashire) roses on his coat.

TALKING TO TREES

Bartle Grove, an eight-acre patch of wild woodland near Northallerton, was bought in 1985 by the Sacred Tree Trust, a registered charity set up to encourage people to commune with trees and tap their alleged therapeutic properties.

There are, it seems, various ways by which this can be achieved. You can simply tell your troubles to the tree. You can sit with your back to it and experience rejuvenation. You can press your forehead (which the ancients called The Third Eye) against it and feel an inner glow.

Centuries ago the locals of Bartle Grove (also known as Woodhead Gill) were said to have been terrorised by a creature called the Sockburn Worm, presumably a dragon. There were also tales of a hobgoblin that wreaked vengeance on anyone who despoiled the area. Before the Trust took over, some trees were chopped down and one of the workmen responsible sat on a log to drink a cup of tea. He reportedly died on the spot for no apparent reason.

COOL

Operated by a pedal, a wooden hand projecting from a Ripon Cathedral organ loft would beat out the time.

❋ ❋ ❋

PALACE OF NUDES

As far back as 1890 posters outside the City Varieties theatre in Leeds were announcing the appearance of a lady known as La Milo, 'wearing only a smile'. She was also billed as The Inimitable Breathing Marble. Off-stage she was Pansy Montague, an Australian who posed 'for art's sake'. Petite and buxom, she apparently appeared completely nude, her body coated with an enamel-like substance. Her various poses included 'Hebe, the Goddess of Youth', 'Sappho', 'Venus de Milo', 'Maidenhood' and 'Diana'. In between poses, her husband-cum-manager made lightning sketches of local personalities under the stage name of Cruickshank (presumably conscious that Charles Dickens' famous illustrator, George Cruickshank, had died twelve years earlier and could hardly sue).

La Milo's appearance confirms that the theatre, which claims to be the country's oldest music-hall, was also a pioneer of stage nudity.

Tucked down a little passage, as if in mock humility, behind a row of shops, the City Varieties owes its conception to Charles Thornton, who, in 1857, became landlord of the White Swan (inevitably known as the Mucky Duck), a pub dating back to the late eighteenth century when artistes were ready to perform on ale-sodden straw for a pint and a penny. Thornton rebuilt the inn as a music-hall, retaining the pub licence for the vaults. The new theatre opened under the name White Swan Varieties in June, 1865, with the 'Brothers Daniel, singers and entertainers' and a starry supporting company. In years to come the theatre, now billed as Thornton's Music Hall and Fashionable Lounge, was patronised by the city's élite. Ladies were admitted free if accompanied by gentlemen, and drinks were served in the auditorium, which must have made for a suitably raucous atmosphere. By the 1870s competition had become so fierce that Thornton quit the music-hall business and built a shopping arcade that still bears his name on a site once the scene of cock-fights. The theatre was put up for auction, but withdrawn when a laughable bid of only £10,000 was received. Eventually, it was bought by an entrepreneur named Jack Stansfield who vaingloriously reopened it as Stansfield's Varieties. He did not stay very long, however, and over the next two decades owners came and went with monotonous regularity. One was a Mr Merritt, who built a new entrance on the Headrow, the city's main thoroughfare. A successor was Joe Lawrence, father of Vesta Victoria, the music-hall star. In 1897 an eight-year-old Charlie Chaplin made his stage debut at the Varieties with the Eight Lancashire Lads, a team of clog-dancers.

When a rumour spread that the Varieties was to be converted into a warehouse, Fred Wood, landlord of The Tapps hotel in Bishopgate Street, where Dan Leno had appeared, stepped in as its saviour, reopening it in 1898 with a comic, Alec Hurley, who was to marry the renowned Marie Lloyd, topping the bill. The Prince of Wales (later Edward VII) often slipped away from boring aristocratic parties at Harewood House in Leeds to spend an evening, incognito, in a curtained box at the theatre. In 1902 the Varieties was given a facelift, which included installation of electric lighting, and twice-nightly shows were introduced. When Wood died, the Varieties was sold by auction and continued to provide its menu of popular light entertainment. The theatre became the City Palace of Varieties in 1905.

In 1941 it was bought by Harry Josephs, who gave future stars such as local lad Frankie Vaughan and Max Bygraves their first breaks. Meanwhile the theatre built up a reputation for the awful puns and word-plays in the titles of its risqué shows: *Strip, Strip, Hooray*; *Eves Without Leaves*; *Halt! Who Goes Bare?* and *Shake It From Here*. Some of the most famous strippers cavorted on its boards and soldiers on leave would make a bee-line for the old place to see such performers as Jane and Phyllis (Peek-a-Boo) Dixie. In 1954 the BBC agreed to televise its series *The Good Old Days* from the City Varieties, which, at a cost of thousands of pounds, was restored to something resembling its erstwhile glory, with new curtains, new spotlights and other fittings, and the erection of a chairman's rostrum. Charlie Chester was the show's first chairman. Under the gavel of Leonard Sachs, the theatre achieved nationwide fame not only for its artistes but also for audiences who rolled up in Edwardian costumes.

In view of its age, it is not surprising to learn that the City Varieties boasts a couple of ghosts, one a female singer holding a candelabra aloft, the other an old-time pianist, both reportedly seen in 1970 by a watchman. There is also a mystery about the coat of arms over the proscenium arch. Nobody knows how it got there, though one not altogether unlikely tale is that it was bestowed by one of its most satisfied customers, Edward VII. Even more baffling are the underground passages said to extend for great distances (one the two miles to Kirkstall Abbey) beneath the building, which is now officially scheduled as being of special architectural interest.

THE MAKING OF WOOLOPOLIS

Little Germany is a Bradford nook that takes its name from the nineteenth-century German-Jewish emigrés who helped transform the city into the textile trade's world centre. They built their tall warehouses in this tiny hillside enclave just off the city centre and became Bradford's first merchant princes, linking their salesman-ship skills to their Yorkshire colleagues' craftsmanship to capture international markets. They also changed the nature of Bradford by putting money into hospitals, schools and welfare schemes, and built the city's present Reform Synagogue. In 1851 two of them, Jacob Behrens and Jacob Unna, founded the Bradford Chamber of

Commerce. A school Behrens established for his children developed into Bradford Grammar School. A contemporary, Julius Delius, who specialised in worsteds, helped arrange local Hallé Orchestra concerts, though it was his son, Frederick, the composer, who made the family name famous. Victor Edelstein, whose business flourished for more than thirty years, became Bradford's first German consul, while Jacob Moser, who had spent most of his formative years learning Hebrew, became the city's Lord Mayor and chief magistrate. The packing-rooms of the warehouse built by Moritz Rothenstein, who arrived in Bradford in 1859, eventually became a picturesque subject for Eric Gill, the engraver. The merchant's son, Sir William Rothenstein, portrait painter and principal of the Royal College of Art, suggested in his memoirs that almost as exciting as a night at the pantomime was a visit to his father's warehouse, 'a place, to us children, of endless interest'. He was particularly intrigued by 'a great steam-engine', cutting machines, bales piled to the ceiling and 'one room where beautiful labels, richly ornamented with gold, were attached to patterns'. In the streets of Little Germany could be heard the rumble of heavily-laden, horse-drawn carts carrying goods to and from the dyeworks and manufacturers, and a strange amalgam of foreign accents and Yorkshire dialects. Being men of artistic sensibilities, the merchants built their warehouses in an ornate style, with gargoyles, pillars and extravagant carvings. One boasts a ship's anchors over the doorway to indicate overseas trade. Generally, development was piecemeal, with odd buildings often standing in splendid isolation as they dominated the skyline. There was even a Continental café, and, years later, J.B. Priestley wrote of growing up with a background of strange-sounding names.

Because of its architecture and historical importance, with fifty-five listed buildings, Little Germany is now on Bradford's heritage trail, and has been designated both as a conservation and a commercial development area. Many sooty buildings have been sandblasted, revealing honey-coloured stones. Narrow streets that once echoed to the hoof-beats of merchants' horses with their heavy, brass-ornamented collars, have been refurbished with attractive, Victorian-style lamp standards. In 2000 some hundred developers from around the country visited the area and were encouraged to invest in Little Germany's future. Ideas included the building of houses and the opening of restaurants and bars.

Oddly enough, Yorkshire also has a Little Denmark, a few square miles of countryside in the east of the county that takes its name from its link with the Scandinavians who colonised it about 1,200 years ago. Its 'capital' is the village of Bempton, a crowded cluster of cottages in narrow, winding streets, with a large green.

CUCKOO!

In Marsden, near Huddersfield, there is a legend that, many years ago, not-too-bright villagers tried to capture the first cuckoo of spring, believing it would bring eternal good weather. They went about the job by building a wall around the bird, but, as they neared completion, the pesky creature flew away. The event is now celebrated by an annual cuckoo festival in Marsden, featuring a street procession, a giant model of a cuckoo and children wearing cuckoo hats.

HERE COMES THE PRINCE

One of the most outstanding features of Leeds is the statue in the central City Square of the Black Prince mounted on a horse with one front foreleg raised. Edward the Black Prince was also called Edward of Woodstock, Prince D'Aquitaine, Prince of Wales, Duke of Cornwall and Earl of Chester. In none of his titles was Leeds mentioned – with good reason, since he had no link with the Yorkshire city. Why then was he chosen to become one of its permanent adornments? He was, in fact, selected by a former Lord Mayor of Leeds, Colonel Walter Harding, as a figure of nobility reflecting the glory of Leeds which had achieved its city status only a decade earlier.

In 1902 Harding commissioned the bronze statue from Thomas Brooke, a Royal Academician (later knighted). It was cast in Belgium. On its completion several months later, it was shipped in a crate from Antwerp to Hull docks, whence it was to be ferried by canal barge to Leeds. Strict orders were given that it must at all times be kept upright. But when loaded at Antwerp it landed on its side on the steamer deck. On arrival at Hull, it was deposited on the wharf in a similar undignified position. The canal agent asked the dock authority to ensure that the crate was raised to a vertical position before being placed on a barge. The authority refused, unless they were indemnified, and as the agent either could or would not accept such a responsibility, Harding agreed to go to Hull with the canal's own engineer to supervise the operation. The engineer, Henry Pickard, discovered that the Prince's horse was attached to the base by three of its hooves and that their fetlocks appeared rather weak. He decided, however, that the designer would have taken into account the strain that would be placed on the fetlocks by wind pressure when the statue was erected. He approved the lifting of the statue and indemnified the dock authority for the use of its steam crane. With a disconcertingly loud creak, the crate was raised to the vertical. It was now realised that, in the side on which it had lain on the wharf, there was a large inspection manhole. Pickard crawled in and, to his relief, found the structure undamaged. The colonel declined an invitation to scramble in and check for himself, perhaps considering this beneath the dignity of a former Lord Mayor.

On the journey to Leeds, the barge carrying the Prince was cheered on its way by canal workers on the banks. When the statue finally arrived, it was carried to the City Square in a horse-drawn wagon. After it had been erected safely without even a chip on its surface, the canal management munificently waived its charges. After the Black Prince had been formally presented to Leeds, the colonel was awarded the freedom of the city.

CHAPTER 4

AT WAR

TOO MUCH NOISE OUTSIDE

The Sheffield blitz is one of the most enduring memories of the city's elder citizens. But through the harrowing reminiscences glimpses of humour gleam. The story is told, for instance, of a shot down German pilot led to a police station by two angry fire-watchers. He asked if he might smoke. The reply, after a pause for thought, was, 'Yes – but tha' smokes thi' own.' Another tale is of a policeman who, after rescuing people trapped in a cellar, eventually crawled out covered in mud, grease, plaster and brick fragments. 'You're a mess,' said an air-raid warden. 'Yes,' said the constable. 'That's the worst of navy blue. It shows every little stain.' During one raid more than half the patrons at the Electra Picture Palace remained in their seats. As the bombs fell nearer and nearer the cinema, the projectionist felt he had no choice. He turned up the volume of the war film being screened to try to drown the unwelcome noise outside.

As the English port nearest to Germany, Hull had particularly tragic experiences of the Luftwaffe's indiscriminate wrath, and proud citizens were miffed by London newspapers that, thanks to the censors, never named the city, simply reporting: 'Enemy raiders were again reported over a northeastern port last night.' Robert G. Tarran, who was Hull's sheriff and chief air-raid warden, wrote to the authorities in London: 'It is bad enough to be bombed, and anybody who says he likes it is a liar. But we ought at least to get credit for it.' A *New Yorker* journalist, A.J. Liebling, who visited the city, told of hearing air-raid sirens: 'All three of my hosts seemed pleased, as if the sound justified the reputation of Hull as the air-raid metropolis of England.' An official said: 'I'll drive around slowly for a few minutes so you can observe the reactions of the populace. You will please notice how Jerry has got our wind up.' Liebling wrote: 'This last remark was Yorkshire irony, which has the same gossamer quality as Yorkshire pudding.' The official showed Liebling a large-scale map of Hull covered with pins with heads of various colours, the different hues representing incendiary bombs, oil bombs, parachute bombs, high explosive bombs etc. 'The idea at first', said the official, 'was to mark every site of bomb damage, but along about last March we found that there were places where we had no room to stick in another pin and besides, the supply of pins was getting to be a problem, so we gave it up.' On a visit to a pub, Liebling found two soldiers playing darts on a board over which hung a sign reading, 'Game Postponed at Gunfire.'

One of the most mysterious air raids occurred at noon on 12 September, 1940, when a Junker 88 dropped three bombs over Harrogate's appropriately named Majestic Hotel. The first lodged on the fifth floor but failed to explode. The second hit the gardens, killing the commissionaire's wife. The third demolished a nearby villa. The first was eventually defused by bomb disposal experts. If it had exploded, it would have blown the hotel to pieces. Even bearing in mind the indiscriminate bombing for which the Luftwaffe was notorious, local people were puzzled by the attack, which appeared to have been deliberately planned. An intriguing explanation was put forward by the tabloid *Daily Graphic*, which recalled a night in 1938 when the head waiter, a stickler for protocol, refused admission to a group of young Germans in town for an air show, their sin being that they were not wearing the obligatory evening dress. The attack, surmised the *Graphic*, might well have been carried out as an act of revenge by those three young Germans.

The scene now moves 140 miles to the Buckinghamshire town of High Wycombe and Hughenden Manor, once the home of Benjamin Disraeli. During the war the house became a Royal Observer Corps base where aerial reconnaissance photographs were interpreted. In 1946, a National Serviceman in the great house stumbled across a list of British targets prepared by the German High Command. One of the most important was

Harrogate, with two specific buildings marked for destruction: the Majestic and the Esplanade Hotels, both identified as Air Ministry staff quarters. The pilot was even warned to expect 'strong flak protection'. Unfortunately for the Nazis, the instructions contained two rather significant errors. First, the Air Ministry did *not* occupy the Majestic. Second, there was no Esplanade Hotel. Thère still isn't.

※ ※ ※

BLOODY YORKSHIRE

One of the most decisive battles of the Wars of the Roses was fought at Towton, midway between Leeds and York, resulting in Edward, Duke of York, becoming Edward IV of England. Twenty-eight thousand died in what may have been the bloodiest battle on English soil. It is commemorated by a cross at the roadside between Towton and Saxton. A mound to the north of Saxton church marks a communal grave, not far from the tomb of the Lancastrian leader, Lord Dacre, said to have been shot by a boy in a tree as he stopped to drink. There is a traditional claim that Dacre was buried sitting on his horse, and when his grave was opened in the nineteenth century, an upright skeleton was found, with horse bones beneath.

Less than ten miles from Towton is Marston Moor, where, two centuries later, a crucial English Civil War battle was fought. It was the first major defeat of the Royalists, who lost up to 4,000 men. According to the Earl of Clarendon, a noted seventeenth-century historian of the Civil War, there were 'more sharp skirmishes and more notable battles' in Yorkshire than in the whole of the rest of the kingdom. It has even been argued that the War began not at Nottingham, where Charles I first raised his standard against the Parliamentarians, but at the strategically important port of Hull, where the town's Parliamentary governor, Sir John Hotham, locked the gates against the king, thus denying him access to munitions held there. The Parliamentary army's commander-in-chief was a Yorkshireman, Sir Thomas Fairfax, born at Denton, near Ilkley. At his home in Nun Appleton, near York, he achieved fame for the quality of the white horses he bred and later rode into battle. When the rift between Parliament and Charles I became acute, Fairfax was chosen to present a petition to the king at York. Sir Thomas and a cousin followed Charles through a field packed with spectators. Clearly intending to avoid and snub the two men, the king rode to greet his supporters. Fairfax grabbed the monarch's bridle in an attempt to force him to listen, but this startled the horse, which reared up, making it appear that Charles was about to ride Fairfax down. Fairfax, however, managed to swivel away from the horse's hooves and present the petition. Observers interpreted the incident as a typical abuse of royal power, thus increasing Fairfax's popularity.

Bradford, then a small town with tiny cloth-making settlements and a few small coal-mines, became an important centre of Parliamentary support. When it was threatened by a Royalist incursion, sharpshooters fired at them from the tower of the parish church (now Bradford Cathedral) down whose sides woolsacks were hung in an attempt to prevent cannonballs penetrating the stone walls. In desperate hand-to-hand fighting the town's defenders repulsed the attackers, slaughtering officers who begged for quarter (mercy) and stripping them of their clothes and possessions. These acts of savagery became bitterly known as 'Bradford Quarter'. When, seven months later, the Royalists positioned artillery around Bradford, the woolsacks were again suspended from the church tower windows, but accurate gunfire blew them away. The victorious Royalists' commander, the Earl of Newcastle, now had the opportunity to wreak revenge. But, when he had settled down for a night's rest in Bolling Hall, a local mansion (now a museum), his intentions were reputedly softened by the appearance of the ghost of a white lady crying out: 'Pity poor Bradford, pity poor Bradford.' It was even said the Earl and the apparition tussled as he tried to ignore her plaintive cries for mercy. In the event, when Newcastle took control of the town the following day, there was no general massacre, although there was widespread pillage. The next year the Parliamentarians reoccupied Bradford, whose economic recovery was hampered by an outbreak of bubonic plague, which caused the deaths of many citizens already weakened by wartime hardships.

Marston Moor marked the end of the Civil War in Yorkshire. Fairfax's father fled the field when it seemed as though the Royalists would carry the day and rode to the Nun Appleton residence. Finding the house in darkness and no one else there, he simply went to bed, and presumably snored while the battle he was supposed to be partly directing raged on.

✳ ✳ ✳

DEATH AT THE SEASIDE

As custodian of Scarborough Castle, Albert Pickup, with his wife Emily and their children, occupied a house near the twelfth-century fortress. Early on the morning of 16 December, 1914, four months after the outbreak of the First World War, the Pickups were at home when they heard a series of fearful whines and explosions. Incredibly, shells were whistling overhead and crashing into the castle's ten-foot-thick walls. Albert's thirteen-year-old daughter Mildred was so terrified she burst out of the house and ran in her nightgown along the street, where Red Cross workers picked her up. None of her family was hurt, but their donkey was so badly injured she had to be destroyed.

This was one of many incidents on the remarkable day the seaside resort was indiscriminately shelled by German warships in the bay, possibly in an ill-conceived attempt to lure the British Grand Fleet into action and at the same time shock a nation that until now had believed itself impregnable.

When the assault began, citizens dressing or at breakfast rushed to their windows and doors believing they were victims of the worst thunderstorm in living memory. People already in the streets became rooted to the spot, while dray-horses whinnied and shied. Bathers in the South Bay swam ashore, grabbed their clothes and towels, and made for the shelter of the sea wall.

The first target was the War Signal Station on Castle Hill in the castle grounds. The three staff snatched up top secret code-books, charts and papers, raced down the stairs and left the station behind. A moment later, it was blown to pieces. One of the men, fearing enemy forces were about to land, soaked the documents in paraffin. Torched, they were flung, in flames, down a well.

A brazier that centuries ago had served as a warning beacon to ships was battered by a shell, while the castle grounds, favoured by picknickers, were left pocked with shell-cases and shrapnel. A gaping hole was punched into the town's lighthouse, the shell ricocheting into a corner of the Grand Hotel. The hotel suffered thirty-five direct hits that blew apart rooms with the best sea views. All that remained standing in the restaurant was a decanter of wine. Luckily, this being the middle of winter, the hotel had only two guests, both of whom escaped unhurt.

At the Westlands School, where the pupils were tucking into breakfast, the explosions were put down to a violent storm, until a little Belgian girl, who had experienced the horrors of shelling in her own country, cried: 'No! It is cannon!' Seconds later a shell struck the building, shattering windows and destroying desks and blackboards. The children were ushered into the cellars. At Scarborough College, a prep school, the youngsters were dressing when the bombardment began. The headmaster strode through the dormitories, ordering the boys to finish dressing and then go to breakfast. The girls of Queen Margaret's School – among them Winifred Holtby, later to achieve fame as the author of the Yorkshire novel *South Riding* – were at breakfast when they heard a bang they assumed was the sound of someone upstairs falling. As the cannonade continued, the headmistress ordered everyone into the cloakroom, where they were to don their long coats, tam o' shanters and thick boots. 'We're going for a walk in the country till it's over,' she said. The girls ran out, crossed muddy ground littered with broken bottles and crockery, and finally joined a throng of refugees heading for the village of Seamer. One elderly invalid woman was carried there on a chair by three other women of her own age.

At Cayton Bay, the Yorkshire Hussars guarding the waterworks pumping station were ordered to stand to at the sound of the first salvo. The NCOs, however, enjoying breakfast in the station manager's house, were commanded by his wife to sit down and finish their meal before it went cold. A postman was killed on the path leading to the house where he had delivered the morning's mail, and a milkman who refused to give up his round was devastated to see his horse killed. The harbourmaster's wife rushed out of their house with her pet parrot tucked under her arm. Another woman, ordered to leave her home, looked around to see which of her possessions she should save. She left clutching a Christmas pudding. A furniture remover piled refugees into his pantechnicons, while others huddled for shelter in a railway tunnel. The railway station was packed with crowds of people hoping to escape, among them a man in a top hat carrying yet another parrot. Here bureaucracy came into its own, some refugees being refused access to the platforms without tickets. One woman with three small children, who was a shilling short of her fare, was denied a ticket until the crowd made up the difference.

After the attack on Scarborough, the Germans switched their attention to Whitby, where the pupils of St John's Church of England School were marched into the countryside singing, 'It's A Long Way To Tipperary' as shells exploded around them.

During the twenty-five minute bombardment of Scarborough, 500 shells were fired, killing seventeen people, including women and children, injuring more than eighty and causing immense destruction. In eleven minutes the Germans sent 150 shells screaming into Whitby, where three died. At the inquest on a Whitby coastguard and a railwayman, the jury decided to hand their fees to the coastguard's widow. When it was all over, a young man named Tussaud, said to be a descendant of Madame Tussaud, the waxworks maker, visited Whitby, to collect relics of the disaster. A child subsequently born in the port was given the Christian names George (after the King) and Shrapnel (to commemorate the attack 'on our undefended town, so dear to all Yorkshire folk and so famous in history'). Fearing further attacks, a Whitby newspaper urged Scotland Yard to despatch detectives to the town 'to ferret out the spies who every night in and out of our town flash signals to the enemy'. On Christmas Eve the *Whitby Gazette* said the seasonal greeting should be subtly changed from 'Peace on earth, goodwill to men' to 'On earth, peace to men of goodwill.' On New Year's Eve, the bells of Whitby's St Mary's parish church, high on the East Cliff, were silent for the first time in living memory.

❄ ❄ ❄

SLAUGHTER

When the First World War broke out, the idea was put forward that a battalion should be formed consisting entirely of Leeds men who, in view of their similar backgrounds, would feel comfortable with each other. Initially there were sneers about a battalion of pampered men, but this nonsense was soon dismissed out of hand. The Lord Mayor, Sir Edward Bretherton, raised the battalion, a task he found remarkably easy. A Leeds solicitor was appointed commander, and the city council's aldermanic leader became the battalion's first quartermaster. Volunteers of all classes signed up, including older businessmen who lied about their age. Their first training ground was a waterworks site, but the Leeds Pals, as they became known, eventually moved to the bleak moor at Colsterdale in North Yorkshire. They had no uniforms, but these and the equipment they lacked were soon provided by Sir Edward, who became an honorary colonel of the battalion. Training, however, was seriously hampered by the removal of up to 500 men from the ranks for commissions in other units.

After a further spell of training on Salisbury Plain, the Pals set sail from Liverpool for Egypt on a Canadian Pacific liner converted into a transport ship. On their second night in the Mediterranean, they crashed into a small French steamer. Around seventy survivors were picked up, and the ship made for Malta for repairs. The delay, however, enabled the Germans to pick up information about the vessel, and, soon after she left Malta, she had to beat off an attack by two U-boats. The men spent Christmas 1915, in Port Said, where they replaced the Gurkhas guarding the Suez Canal. Early in the New Year they moved into the Sinai desert, where they dug a defensive line of trenches.

When the Germans began their first great attack on Verdun, the Pals received orders to make for France. They sailed from Port Said for Marseilles. After the war one of the men was to write in a *Yorkshire Weekly Post* article: 'The sight of crowds of German prisoners working on the Marseilles docks attracted our attention as we steamed into harbour, and I thought what big fine fellows they were.'

A train journey through the heart of France brought the Pals to the mouth of the Somme. After the sunshine of Egypt, they found themselves in the snow and slush of a French winter. Many men fell ill, and a brigadier died of pneumonia.

The Pals took over a sector of trenches and, as the months passed, it became clear that the sea collision had been a portent of disasters to come. The last day of June 1916 was followed by a beautiful summer night that was transformed into an inferno on the banks of the Somme. Assailed by artillery fire, the Pals spent the night in their battered trenches, waiting anxiously for the order to attack. Their objective was the village of Serre, a quarter of a mile away.

The men went over the top in waves, one staff observer later commenting that it was an action not only deliberate but almost nonchalant: a magnificent display of coolness and discipline. But it was all fruitless. The men were mown down by machine-gun fire, and one party that had reached Serre had to fight their way out again. In the action all the officers but one were killed. Every sergeant-major also perished, and only a handful of the original 800 rank and file survived. They moved back to battalion head-quarters to rest and, within a fortnight, the unit was brought up to a strength of 500 by an influx of new draftees. They were sent back to the line, which they held till the end of the year.

Early in 1917 they found the remains of those who had died a few months earlier. One was Major Booth, a Yorkshire county cricketer, identified by a cigarette case picked up in a shell-hole. It had been presented to him by the MCC as a memento of his team's tour of South Africa.

In another tragic confrontation, the new Pals were practically wiped out. This time 700 men died. But for five days the few who survived clung on to their positions. Pioneers, engineers, drivers, batmen and cooks were ordered into the trenches to beat back fresh offensives. For their bravery they were to receive medals: among them the DCM to Company Sergeant-Major Joe Jones, the champion heavyweight wrestler of Yorkshire.

They held the trenches for some months before being moved to a new sector to free the Second Canadian Division from a terrible slaughter in the dreadful, so-called No Man's Land north of Lens. At the end of March 1918, the Germans made their great bid for Amiens, and the Pals marched two miles to the Somme, where they were relentlessly pushed back.

They fought a desperate rearguard action, leaving the wounded where they fell, in the confusion. Once again they hung on, until only forty-five men remained alive, most of them to receive gallantry medals. Later, defending a railway line, they again fought to the last man and prevented the Germans from breaking through.

After the war, the Leeds City Art Gallery displayed twenty silver cups and other trophies the Pals had won in sporting events while they were in training, including a cross-country championship in France in the dreadful year of 1917.

In his post-war *Yorkshire Weekly Post* article, the former Leeds Pal wrote, in what must have been the greatest understatement of those terrible years: 'We found the conditions in France very trying.'

BEAT OUT THAT RHYTHM

In the officers' mess of Bourlon barracks at Catterick Garrison are six side-drums captured from Napoleon's army shortly before Waterloo. They were taken by the 34th Foot, known as the Cumberland Gentlemen, forerunners of the King's Own Royal Border Regiment, as they marched to the battlefield. Since then the French have made fruitless attempts to have the drums returned. Every year, on the other hand, the regiment receives a letter from the mayor of the Spanish village of Arroyo dos Molinos, where the drums were confiscated, congratulating them on coming to the community's aid. Two Russian drums seized by the Green Howards during the Battle of Alma in the Crimean War are on display in the regimental museum at Richmond.

CHAPTER 5

MYSTERIES

TRAIN TO OBLIVION

Louis Le Prince was a French inventor who, after studying chemistry, specialised in the painting and firing of pottery. In 1866, at the age of twenty-five, he met and became friendly with a Yorkshireman, John Whitley, in Paris, and was invited to Leeds to meet Whitley's family, who ran an engineering firm. Three years later he married John's sister and settled in Leeds, where the couple founded the Park Square school of applied art. In 1881 Le Prince left for New York where he watched a Panorama, a fashionable entertainment that involved painted scenes revolving before an audience. This led to an interest in moving images, and soon afterwards he began experimenting with the possibility of projecting motion pictures. In 1886 he applied for an American patent for a machine, with one or more lenses, and in Europe for patents for a single-lens version. He rented a workshop (demolished in the 1960s) in Woodhouse Lane, Leeds, and by 1888 had constructed two single-lens cameras with paper negative rolls wound into spools that moved intermittently. In his father-in-law's garden in the leafy suburb of Roundhay he carried out early trials and later shot a brief, flickering movie of a horse-tram crossing the cast-iron Leeds Bridge. He made the film at between twelve and twenty frames per second from a window above an ironmonger's in a building that still stands on the bridge's south-east corner. Only twenty frames survive today.

Le Prince's French family had stayed in New York while he tried to perfect his machine, and eagerly awaited the day he would return to demonstrate his miraculous invention to a goggling American public. Before making his trip, however, he visited his brother in Dijon to sort out a domestic matter. When he was ready to leave, his brother accompanied him to the station and watched

Louis Le Prince

him board the Paris train. The forty-eight-year-old Le Prince was never seen again.

Various theories have been propounded to explain his disappearance. One is that he was plagued by debt and, having deliberately vanished, assumed a new identity to avoid his creditors. Another and rather more outlandish suggestion was that he was murdered by agents of Thomas Edison. To the end of her life, his widow insisted he had been disposed of by people who wanted to gain control of the budding motion picture industry.

Whatever the explanation, it is generally agreed that, had his invention proved a commercial success, Le Prince would have become accepted as a pioneer of the movie industry and become a household name. In fact it was Edison who, in 1908, was acknowledged to be the inventor of moving pictures, while Le Prince remains little known. In Leeds, however, he has not been entirely forgotten. On the site of his workship, a BBC TV studio now stands, with two plaques commemorating him inside the building. One was originally on the workshop wall, and the other was unveiled by Richard Attenborough in 1988, when the Leeds International Film Festival re-enacted Le Prince's filming of Leeds Bridge, a century after the event. His American grandson unveiled a plaque on the bridge itself, which also bears a plaque unveiled in 1930 by his daughter, acknowledging his achievement. Le Prince's projectors were held by the Leeds Museum until 1941, when one was destroyed in an air-raid. As all records were also destroyed it cannot be declared with absolute certainty that the remaining projector was a Le Prince original.

THE REAL PHANTOM OF THE OPERA

In January, 1900 the Grand Opera House was opened in Harrogate. In 1967 it was renamed The Harrogate Theatre, but the original title can still be seen on a lighted cupola atop the building. The theatre also has a resident ghost, affectionately known as Alice. Some claim she was an usherette, some a cleaner, others (most commonly) an actress whose rôles dwindled in length as she aged and who may have had an unhappy affair with a colleague. All accounts agree that, whatever she was, she killed herself by jumping from the balcony into the stalls.

Whatever the truth of this, the theatre has seen a number of events that, at the time, seemed to defy rational explanation. In the 1990s an usherette was cleaning the balcony after a pantomime matinée, bent down to pick up an item of litter and suddenly felt extremely cold. Looking up, she saw the whitish-grey shape of a woman hovering in the balcony by the lighting box. When a theatre employee walked into the box to switch on the light, the figure disappeared.

One popular play staged at the theatre was Noel Coward's *Blithe Spirit*, about a mischievous ghost named Elvira. In one scene the maid enters the drawing-room to clear the tea-cups, sees a gramophone apparently playing by itself and drops her tray in terror. When the actress playing the maid walked on, she saw a woman's shape, again whitish-grey, standing on-stage. When the 'maid' dropped her tray it was out of genuine fear.

In March 2000 a technician was working with a lighting designer in the theatre at four in the morning. As they stood on the stage, both saw a pillar of brilliant blue light in front of the circle. It shot across to the other side of the auditorium and hovered there awhile before disappearing. The two spectators were scared out of their wits.

There have been many other accounts of sightings of a woman in a long dress who vanishes and of a woman's head, and of an unaccountable smell of peppermint in the balcony. Alice is also credited with moving tools around and switching lights on and off. She has become so much a part of the theatre's life that, in the autumn of 2000, a chilling play about her, simply titled *Alice*, was staged there.

✻ ✻ ✻

THE FINDING OF MARY JANE

In June 1986 the secretary of the Ilkley and District Arts Federation announced that she had received 'a mysterious but apparently authentic letter' from one Vera Hainsworth, an eighty-six-year-old woman, formerly of Ilkley but now living in Birmingham. Shortly after the First World War, she wrote, her beloved Uncle Ernest swore her to secrecy before telling her a bizarre tale. When he was in his teens, he said, he and his friends had formed an Ilkley archaeological society, primarily interested in Roman remains. On Ilkley Moor they did some digging near what is known as the Druid's Stone. To their surprise, they unearthed a skeleton, which at first they thought to date from the Iron Age, until they discovered an emerald locket inscribed, 'To MJP 1825 with love.' On top of the human remains lay the bones of a large bird. Ernest's friend, a chorister named Jim Smith, wrote a song based on the discovery. This achieved international fame. 'MJP', suggested Ernest, was none other than Mary Jane, the character whose story is told in Yorkshire's anthem *On Ilkla Moor Baht 'At* (trans: *On Ilkley Moor Without A Hat*).

Hitherto, the song was assumed to have been composed in a pub and to be based on a choir outing on the Moor, when a young man slipped away to spoon with his sweetheart, Mary Jane. When he came back, his colleagues chanted that, wandering about without a hat, he was liable to catch a cold, die and become food for the worms, which would be eaten by ducks, in turn dined on by humans. Was the Moor skeleton Mary Jane? Even if the large bird that lay on the human remains were a duck, that would be inconsistent with the lyric, which links the creature not with the girl but with her lover.

The accepted story of the song differs from Uncle Ernest's. The melody – although few Yorkshiremen will admit it – is that of *Cranbrook*, a hymn written by Thomas Clark, a Canterbury cobbler. Despite the tune's Kent provenance, people – especially Yorkshire expatriates – have been coming to Ilkley Moor to sing it since Victorian times, and it is known around the world. The song has been published in a tourists' guide to Ilkley, and one local firm, established in 1869, cashed in on its fame by selling Baht 'At Whisky and Baht 'At Yorkshire Tea-Bread.

Despite the known origin of the melody, there will never be a shortage of historians eager to unearth unexpected sources of the lyric. A 1925 issue of a Workers' Educational Association journal published an article headed, 'Ilkley Moor – A Literary Discovery'. The true source of the Yorkshire anthem, it reported, had been tracked down by an (unidentified) WEA tutor. The song, it appeared, was a debased dialect version of a poem whose style confirmed that it was written by Henry Wadsworth Longfellow, the popular nineteenth-century American poet. The article even goes so far as to quote a long poem in blank, convoluted verse in a style reminiscent of Longfellow's *Hiawatha*:

> *This is the moorland primeval, the far-famed*
> *moorland of Ilkley*
> *Where the breezes blow in the bracken, and*
> *yellow and prickly the gorse grows;*
> *Twixt the valley of Wharfe and the river*
> *that runneth from Skipton . . .*

The poem goes on to tell of one John Smith (a useful name) of Ilkley who one evening wanders off over the Moor, leaving behind friends drinking at the bar of the Blue Boar and singing in dialect:

> *Mirthful were they with song and the fearsome speech of their* *county.*

John's companion, with whom he is 'in amorous rapture' is Mary Jane, 'a maiden modest and buxom' who had lived fifteen years in

Pudsey, who had worked for fifteen years as a cook at the home of a local brewer, and who weighed fifteen stone 'on the scale at the gate of the goods-yard'. Her waist was 'the despair of her lover', but he was so eager to meet her that he had left his hat on his mother's hat-peg. In the chill wind he caught a cold from which he subsequently died, and he now lay in a grave on the edge of the Moor, while his spirit knocked in vain at the gate 'where never a Yorkshireman enters'.

The sinister nature of the Moor is that it is the scene of Yorkshire's oldest and most mysterious carving: a swastika on one of its large boulders. The emblem, despite its current connotations, was, in fact, an ancient symbol supposed to bring good luck. Historians and antiquarians, however, have failed to agree on its significance in Ilkley, perhaps confused by the fact that it is also found in India. There is a suggestion that it could be a relic of a long-forgotten cult. Unfortunately, there are no known songs about it.

❄ ❄ ❄

MAN ON A HORSE

Outside Newby Hall, a mansion near Ripon, stands a marble statue of a warrior on a horse, and beneath them a cowering, prostrate figure. The monument bears a tablet declaring that it was originally built to represent John Sobieski, King of Poland, trampling on a Turkish soldier. If true, this would suggest it commemorates the rout by Sobieski's countrymen of an invading army of the Ottoman Empire, created by Turkish tribes in Anatolia. The statue, the inscription goes on, was subsequently altered to change the identities of both warrior and victim. But how much of this is true?

The story handed down over the centuries is that a certain Sir Robert Vyner bought the original statue in Italy in 1675, took it to London, changed the warrior's head to represent Charles II, and had the Turk recreated as Oliver Cromwell. Vyner then had the statue moved to a spot in the City of London (now the site of the

Mansion House). In 1883 a descendant of Vyner moved it to its present location.

What little knowledge we have of Vyner confirms his artistic background. He was a successful London goldsmith, who, on Charles II's Restoration, presented the English monarch with a new set of Crown Jewels. From then on, he enjoyed a special relationship with Charles, was appointed the King's personal goldsmith, and was subsequently made a baronet. He even loaned increasingly large sums of money to Charles to finance the extravagance of his court. In the event, Vyner lost more than £400,000 (equivalent to around forty million today) that the King failed to repay. Unfazed, Vyner reputedly went on to have the statue reconstructed: an act of supreme loyalty or sycophancy, depending on one's point of view.

In 1737, the City fathers decided to build the Mansion House on the site and advertised the statue for sale. This led to an indignant letter from a citizen on behalf of Vyner's great-nephew, complaining that this was an insult to the late Sir Robert, who had paid not only for the statue itself but also £700 for the eighteen-foot-high pedestal. Sir Robert's heirs would not suffer such abuse, and there could well be a legal prosecution. The great-nephew, also named Robert Vyner, was MP for Lincolnshire, and had bought an estate at Gautby in that county. He now firmly told the City of London's Town Clerk that the statue 'should remain there till wasted or devoured by time'.

His threat discounted, the statue was in fact removed to an 'engine house', where it remained forty years. In 1779 the next Robert Vyner asked permission to take the statue away. This was granted, and he erected it on an island in the ornamental lake at Gautby. Here it stayed until 1883 and the death of the Vyner then in residence. It passed to his brother, whose father had married the heiress to the Newby estate, whither it was removed and where it now stands.

The trouble is that all relevant historical documents make no mention of the statue's origins, or, specifically, of any link with King John Sobieski (who had, indeed, won a victory over the

Turks), or of any alterations. Sobieski was extraordinarily rich, and possessed an amazing collection of rubies, which apparently disappeared. There has even been a legend that they are hidden

inside the horse. Daniel Defoe, in his *Tour Thro' the whole Island of Great Britain*, mentioned the statue, but made no reference to the Polish king. When the statue, still in London, was seen by the compiler of an eighteenth-century art dictionary, he confirmed that it had been made in Italy and brought to this country by Vyner. The horseman's head, however, was unfinished: 'only a block fit to carve'. It was eventually given features, the dictionary reported, by a London sculptor.

Equestrian Statue at Newby Hall, Ripon

(Courtesy of Robin Compton, Newby Hall)

The story of the statue being originally made to honour Sobieski was apparently not mentioned until 1734, some sixty years after it was erected in London. Two years later it was referred to in a faintly contemptuous review of buildings and statues in the capital. The writer does say that it was made for the King of Poland, but adds that it was left on the workmen's hands and bought by the City on the cheap. The Pole was then converted into a Briton and the Turk into Oliver Cromwell.

But there are still doubts about the statue's alleged provenance. One suggestion is that the story arose because the figure being trampled on was wearing a turban. The monument certainly attracted attention. Defoe noted that, on the morning after a lady of the English court gave birth to a child, a cushion reportedly appeared on the statue behind the rider. Pinned to it was a scrap of paper bearing the message, 'Gone for a midwife.' Defoe cautiously added, 'how true it may be, let those who saw it testify.' The only consolation in this miasma of fact and possible fiction is that nobody has ever quibbled about the identity of the horse.

❉ ❉ ❉

BEWITCHED

In 1621 a series of extraordinary events occurred at the Fewston, near Ilkley, home of Edward Fairfax, a distinguished poet. Time and again his two daughters, Helen, who was twenty-one, healthy, and in her father's words, 'free from melancholy', and Elizabeth, aged seven, with pleasant features and a quick wit, would fall into a trance. On their recovery, they would describe encounters they had had with curious individuals and creatures while they were in a sleeplike state. They had seemingly been possessed by demons, summoned, Fairfax believed, by local witches. He subsequently produced an account of these incidents under the title *Daemonologia*, so meticulous it resembled the casebook notes of a latter-day psychiatrist.

It all began shortly before supper-time on Sunday 28 October when Helen was sent into the parlour to poke the fire. She was absent so long that her brother William went to see what had kept her. He found her lying on the floor in what we would now call a cataleptic condition. He picked her up but could not revive her. For several hours she appeared to be lifeless, until finally recovering consciousness. While in her trance, she said, she found herself in a Leeds church listening to the preacher's sermon. During trances on subsequent days she conversed, she reported, with family members who had died many years previously. At dawn six days after the first episode, she was lying in Fairfax's room when she suddenly cried out: 'Oh, I am poisoned.' Her mother, clearly a practical person, inquired: 'What with?' Helen made the strange reply that a white cat had lain on her, drawn out her breath, and left in her mouth and throat 'so filthy a smell that it doth poison me'. Her family tried to persuade her that she had been day-dreaming, but during future trances, as if in confirmation of her story, she vomited blood.

On 14 November Helen saw a black dog at her bedside, and, after a brief sleep, the apparition of a young gentleman wearing a hat with a gold band and a fashionable ruff, who promptly pro-posed marriage. When she reasonably asked who he was, he said, 'A prince', and promised that, if she eloped with him, he would make her queen of England 'and all the world'. She declined this generous offer, and repeated her inquiry more forcefully: 'In the name of God, what are you?' This irked the young man, who for-bade her to mention God's name. Helen made the possibly obvi-ous deduction: 'You are the devil.' The gentleman then vanished, but returned with a well-dressed woman he said was his wife, whom he would guarantee to leave, should Helen join him. She still declined. The man left, but returned once more holding a knife, with which Helen, he said, must kill herself.

When she insisted she would have none of this, he advised her to remove a pin from her clothes and put it in her mouth. 'I have no pins,' she responded. 'My clothes are sewed.' The man said, 'Yes, you have a great pin in your petticoat.' This was true. At this point, Alexander Cooke, the vicar of Leeds, appeared in the room in his regulation gown and breeches. Taking a parchment volume from under his arm, he began to read prayers, and bade Helen not to be afraid: hearing which, the stranger departed.

The following day Helen dozed off in the kitchen and slipped again into a trance. When the young man rematerialised, she began to say, 'Begone, Satan' but he interrupted with a demand that she either jump out of the window or meet him in the court-yard. He also presented her with a dagger and a red horse with a green saddle, and suggested she mount and ride off with him. 'Dost thou carry carry folk to hell on horseback?' asked Helen. 'Well, let them ride to hell who will, for I will go on foot to heaven.' The man then cut off the horse's head, but said he could re-attach it, if Helen agreed to ride with him. His next trick was to turn into a multi-horned beast. In the manner of Red Riding Hood, the girl exclaimed: 'O, what terrible horns hast thou!' Apparently discouraged by this reaction, he then turned himself into, first, a calf, and then a little dog, asking her to open her mouth and let him into her body. If she obeyed, he would then be in a position to rule the world. 'Now thou art a dog, if I had a staff I would kill thee,' Helen retorted. In what appeared a final act of desperation, he filled the kitchen with fire. Unimpressed, Helen said: 'I neither care for thee nor thy fire.' The man left.

The next evening Helen sat up late, unwilling to go to bed, as the spirit, or whatever it was, had promised to return. Her brother and a woman servant kept watch with her. She eventually fell asleep and, predictably, went into yet another trance. When her father went to her, she awoke and said a red cat had lain on her.

Helen's mother then recalled a visit she had received a few days earlier from Margaret Waite, a local widow whose husband had been hanged for theft and who herself had a reputation for theft and witchcraft. Mrs Fairfax had provided Margaret with some corn, for which the disreputable woman had paid a penny. A few days later she returned to ask for the penny's return, arguing that it kept her from dreaming. It was easily recognisable, she pointed out, as it had a hole through which she would run a thread to hang it around her neck. On hearing this statement, one of Fairfax's servants burst out laughing, and Margaret stamped out in a fury and without her precious penny. Now Fairfax decided that the penny had been some kind of magic talisman that had been put to evil use and had been responsible for Helen's weird experiences.

His wife had locked the penny in a desk in the parlour. But when they opened it, there was no sign of the coin. Meanwhile the servant who had laughed developed an infirmity in his legs. Subsequently Helen unlocked the desk again and found the penny lying on one of its shelves. 'Whereupon,' wrote Fairfax, 'I took it and put brimstone upon it, and so thrust it into the midst of the fire, which was so vehement that it moved Mr Smithson [the vicar of Fewston, who was visiting] to say, "I warrant you it will trouble you no more," and we all thought it to be molten and consumed, yet on Sunday following, 2nd December, the penny again lay in sight before the fire . . . Then I took it and with brimstone and fire dissolved it, and beat it to powder on a stone.'

The next Sunday both his daughters experienced trances in which they saw two cats fighting viciously, one finally grabbing Helen's throat with its forepaws. The animals chased each other into the oven and out of the house. Despite her travails, Helen laughed.

When the trances continued, the family felt matters had gone too far. Justices were persuaded to arrest six local women on witchcraft charges. They were Margaret Waite, whose familiar was said to be a black, deformed, rough-haired creature of unknown species; her 'impudent and lewd' daughter, who had a white cat with a black spot; Jennit Dibble, an elderly widow whose witchlike propensities were said to have been inherited; her daughter Margaret, a widow whose companion was a yellow bird as large as a crow; Elizabeth Fletcher, whose wealthy neighbours so feared her they lit her fires and gave her meat; and a woman named Elizabeth Dickenson, who had owned a white cat named Fillie for twenty years. Local people blamed these women for lost possessions, especially milk-cows, and, for advice on how to cope with these much-hated ladies, would consult a soothsayer. 'So little is the truth of the Christian religion known in these wild places and among this rude people – on whose ignorance God have mercy!' wrote Fairfax, somewhat hypocritically as, despite his denials, he was clearly as superstitious as his less educated neighbours.

The women appeared at York Assizes, where it was alleged that they had bewitched Fairfax's children. But the judge ruled that, as the children were alive, there were no legal grounds for the women's conviction. This, wrote Fairfax, was unfair. He claimed that many wiser men than he were stupefied by the result of these proceedings.

The trances continued.

AMY, ENIGMATIC AMY

On the cold, foggy afternoon of 5 January 1941, a British aircraft and a parachute from which dangled the small figure of a woman, plunged into the Thames estuary, close to a convoy menaced by German bombers. Lieutenant Commander Walter Fletcher, commanding a Naval trawler, HMS *Haslemere*, jumped into the rough sea in a rescue attempt. But when the ship heaved, the woman disappeared beneath the icy waves. Fletcher was pulled aboard his vessel, but died soon afterwards.

The woman was the Hull aviator, Amy Johnson, and for six decades the manner of her death has remained a mystery. At the time Amy was piloting a plane of the Air Transport Auxiliary (ATA), composed of experienced pilots who, for various reasons, were ineligible for the RAF. Their main job was to ferry planes from the factories in which they were built to RAF bases. On the day she died, Amy – who, years later, was said to have had a vivid personality but problematic flying skills – had taken off from Prestwick in Scotland for Kidlington, Oxfordshire, with an overnight stop at the Squires Gate airfield in Blackpool.

Amy's motto had always been, 'Be careful.' Why, then, had her innate caution let her down? Had her plane's wings iced over? Amy had been well off-course. Why? Had her compass given an inaccurate reading? Gunfire had been reported in the area. Did this mean an enemy plane had shot her down? Or had she collided with another aircraft? Had she simply run out of petrol or had engine trouble?

The oddest aspect of the incident was a report by members of the *Haslemere*'s crew that they had seen another figure – apparently a man's – in the water before Commander Fletcher had leapt in to try to save her. Who, then, was this Mr X? Was he an enemy pilot who had been shot down? Or, in the yellow fog, had Amy's baggage been mistaken for a man?

At the time and over the years there has been intense speculation about the real purpose of Amy's flight, about which there was some official reticence. One story, since discounted, was that she had taken off in impossibly bad weather to attend a party at Hatfield, Hertfordshire, celebrating the ATA women's section's first anniversary.

Back home in Hull, Amy's family were not even able to obtain a formal death certificate, which, it seems, was only granted in the case of a death 'alleged to have occurred in consequence of war operations'. ATA duties were apparently ruled out.

The officer commanding the women's section of the ferry pilots' pool at Hatfield Aerodrome, had at first written to Amy's father that 'Amy, with a passenger, was flying to an aerodrome in the South of England.' But the number of deaths was later changed from two to one. The popular press, however, felt there was a story to be unearthed about a secret liaison with a man who had been Amy's unauthorised passenger. The *Daily Express* asked: 'Where did Amy pick up Mr X?'

A lawyer who had been a First World War undercover agent – and was later to become president of the Law Society – was assigned to find evidence that would satisfy the Probate Court of Amy's death. He saw his task, however, as rather more subtle: to scotch 'malicious rumours' about her, one being that she had been attempting to smuggle a man into Europe (an act that could have been construed as treasonable). Years later, a woman named Alison King, who had served as an operations officer on the ATA ground staff at Hatfield, suggested that Mr X might well have been a Free Frenchman. But the job of flying Allied agents into France was confined to service pilots in small Lysander aircraft. The mystery has been mulled over for some sixty years, and as late as 2000 a Yorkshire octogenarian who, as an RAF mechanic at Squires Gate, had readied Amy's plane for take-off, claimed he knew the real reason for her disappearance, and spoke of the strange disappearance of Air Ministry telegrams about her.

Amy Johnson was the eldest daughter of a Hull herring importer, and granddaughter of a former mayor of the city. Another grandfather was a Dane named Jorgensen, who sailed to Hull at sixteen, settled in England, and changed his name to Johnson. Amy attended Hull's Boulevard Secondary School (later

Kingston High), where she preferred the company of boys to that of her own sex. A sporty girl, she tended to be a show-off in the gymnasium, but when a cricket ball smashed into her mouth, her front teeth had to be replaced by dentures. Mocked by schoolmates, she frequently played truant, and wandered alone across the Yorkshire moors. On her first visit to a cinema she sat twice through a newsreel about a plane, and decided on the spot that one day she would learn to fly.

JOHNSONIANA.

Punch cartoon comparing Amy Johnson's fame with Dr Samuel Johnson's.
(Courtesy of Punch Ltd)

When she took a place at Sheffield University, her family presumed she would become a teacher, but despite her BA there was a distinct change of plan. With the flying craze at its peak, Amy kept the promise to herself and took flying lessons, overcoming the prejudice of sexist ground engineers with whom she worked without pay until she qualified. On 5 May 1930, with no wider experience than a flight to Hull from London, she set off on her spectacular and historic attempt to break the light aeroplane record in a solo flight to Australia in a tiny Moth named Jason after her father's trademark. She reached Karachi in six days, breaking the record for that distance, but failed to break the record to Port Darwin, where she did not arrive until 24 May. Undaunted, she flew on to Brisbane, where, either through weariness or inexperience or a combination of both, she overshot the aerodrome and wrecked the plane. But her flight was so astonishing the British public rolled over in ecstasy. She was awarded the CBE, the *Daily Mail* made her a gift of £10,000, a simple-minded song, 'Amy, Wonderful Amy', hit the air-waves, her uncle in Leeds wrote another ditty called 'The Lone

Dove', and a *Punch* cartoon titled 'Johnsonia' linked her fame with Dr Samuel Johnson's. She had a brief marriage to Jim Mollison, an American pilot and playboy. One day she told a friend: 'I know where I shall finish up – in the drink.'

In 1959 her father donated her trophies and mementoes – including her flying suit, an Australian boomerang and the pigskin flight bag found floating in the water when she plunged to her death – to Bridlington Corporation, which has devoted a special room at the Sewerby Hall Art Gallery and Museum to her memory. There is also a statue of Amy in Prospect Square in her native city. In 1982 a bizarre memorial to the aviatrix was discovered in the unlikeliest of locations. It was a crude sketch of a plane with Amy's name superimposed, carved on the pavement leading to the Haworth parsonage, home of the Brontë sisters. Eventually it was identified by a sixty-year-old citizen as one he had chipped as a child, with his father's chisel, on the pavement in front of his house during the outburst of Johnson mania. When the street was knocked down, the flagstones were sold by the demolition firm involved, and the one bearing the picture finished up on the path to the parsonage. It may have been alarmingly anachronistic, but it demonstrated the hold Amy Johnson once had over an exuberant British public.

THE SOUND OF VICARAGE MUSIC

Any violinist would treasure a Stradivarius. But, while not in the same class, a Tweedale fiddle is also an instrument that has earned some respect. This is scarcely surprising, since, if its maker was to be believed, its creation was inspired by Stradivari's ghost.

The Revd Charles Tweedale, a vicar of Weston, near Ilkley, was a part-time astronomer and violin-maker, married to a self-declared psychic. The couple were friends of Sir Arthur Conan Doyle, notorious for his gullibility when it came to what was described as spiritualism. Tweedale himself was convinced that the secret of the

Strad's beautiful sounds lay in its varnish, and over half a century devoted countless hours to researching its possible constituents, achieving what he believed to be eventual success in the 1930s. The story of how he made his crucial discovery had begun in 1901 when the Tweedales moved into their three-storey vicarage. Very soon afterwards, if Charles's account is to be believed, strange events began to occur with monotonous regularity. Strangest of all was the constant appearance of the spirit of the Italian master, Stradivari, wearing a skull-cap, long girdled cassock, and shoes with turned-up toes. Sometimes he was accompanied by a smiling black cat that, after it had made its presence known, would melt away. It was Stradivari, recorded Tweedale in his enormous work *News From The Next World* (published in 1940), who personally encouraged him in his endeavours.

His odd experiences had first manifested themselves many years earlier. In his youth he had taught himself to play a violin made by his grandfather. One autumn evening he was playing from an instruction book, and had paused reflectively with the fiddle still under his chin, when he felt someone grab and tug the bow with some impatience. No one else was in the gas-lit room. His investigations into Stradivari's varnish began a few years later, and in 1905 the vicar allowed a London psychic, who did not know him from Adam, to examine his handwriting. 'This man,' she pronounced, 'is engaged on a problem which is almost insoluble.' Not long afterwards Tweedale visited a Newcastle-on-Tyne bookseller, who claimed clairvoyant powers and who allegedly informed the vicar: 'There is an old man with you, an Italian . . . who is teaching you something, but I cannot make out what it is.'

Tweedale always denied that his vicarage was haunted, attributing the welter of odd events there to his wife's paranormal powers. A typical incident involved the sound of music seeping from the top of a wardrobe and resembling that of a music-box, though none was in the house. On another occasion, after Stradivari had made one of his customary walkabouts, Tweedale heard a chord strummed on a fiddle hanging on a wall behind him as he sat alone in his study.

When Stradivari's spirit appeared, it rarely minced words. It would often exclaim, 'I am he, he, he.' One day in 1925, Tweedale's wife and daughter were sitting in the greenhouse with a ouija board when Stradivari spelled out his name, to ensure there was no mistake about his identity. The following winter, a so-called psychic photographer took some family pictures in the vicarage. On three plates appeared the 'fine face' of a bearded man, closely resembling published illustrations of Stradivari.

Tweedale received a discouraging letter from one Strad owner reporting: 'I have heard only two violins which I believe equal to mine, one being the Stradivari at present owned by Fritz Kreisler.' Deeming this a challenge, the vicar sent the correspondent one of his own fiddles. The recipient wrote back: 'I have never played on a violin for which less than two thousand was being asked, which was as gratifying and as responsive as your violin.' On New Year's Day 1930, the old Italian materialised to congratulate his pupil on this compliment.

The vicar recorded his attempts to recreate the Strad varnish: 'Filled with enthusiasm and attracted by the romance that surrounded the whole subject, I sat at the bench, gouge and chisel in hand, and compounded innumerable combinations with dragon's blood [a red resin] and gamboge [a yellow gum resin].' In 1937, within a few weeks of the bicentary of Stradivari's death, he claimed to have succeeded. He jubilantly sent the news to the Italian dictator Mussolini, but received no personal reply.

Seven years earlier, a directory of violin-makers had paid tribute to Tweedale's achievements. Praising his general workmanship, it said his instruments also had a 'robust aspect'. In 1960 the *Universal Dictionary of Violin and Bow-Makers* confirmed that the late vicar had received 'the most flattering testimonials' from musicians. Today a Tweedale violin can be identified by its distinctive label: the clergyman's photograph and, in the corners, a telescope (acknowledging his interest in astronomy), a camera, a violin and a lathe.

A QUEEN RETURNS

After Mary Queen of Scots was deposed, she unwisely sought refuge in England, where Queen Elizabeth I, employing a series of excuses connected with the murder of Mary's second husband, kept her imprisoned for the rest of her life. One of her places of incarceration was Bolton Castle in Wensleydale, where she arrived in July 1568 and stayed for about six months. Under supervision, she was allowed to visit various locations in the area, among them Nappa Hall, near Askrigg, where she slept. A story is told that, in 1878, more than three centuries after the visit, a young girl who was a guest at the Hall was playing hide-and-seek in the dark foyer with the owner's daughter when she became aware of a beautifully dressed female figure. Thinking it was a family friend, she ran after the woman and reached out to touch her dress. It was velvet and in the Tudor style. The figure also wore a small hat.

When the woman turned to confront the little girl, her face was revealed. It was, the girl said later, soft and lovely. After staring at the child for a few moments, the lady walked away and disappeared through a doorway leading to a winding staircase. The stairs led to a turret in the west tower containing the room in which Mary had once slumbered. When the child was shown a portrait of Mary, she confirmed this was the woman she had encountered.

There have been several other sightings of Mary's ghost, variously described as The Blue Lady and The Grey Lady. In the winter of 1908 she was seen at Temple Newsam, the Leeds stately home (where Mary's murdered husband is said to have been born) by the Earl of Halifax. A woman with a shawl around her shoulders, he claimed, crossed his bedroom in the firelight and vanished into the next room.

The Nappa Hall bed in which Mary slept is no longer there. One rumour is that it now graces a bed-and-breakfast establishment.

VANISHING TRICK

The victory of Victor Grayson, the young, handsome and dynamic Labour candidate in the Colne Valley by-election of 1907, was a remarkable affair. This had been thought of as a safe Liberal seat. Moreover, Grayson was a firebrand uncomfortably far to the left of his Parliamentary colleagues. National newspapers shuddered that his election presaged a Red revolution and that British politics would never be the same. In the event, he had no significant influence on the public weal during his three years as an MP. Yet his name was to be remembered until the end of the century and beyond.

Born on 5 September 1881, Grayson was the son of a Yorkshire soldier named Dickenson, said to have deserted to marry, changed his name to Grayson, and settled down to work in Liverpool as a carpenter. The boy Victor had a serious speech impediment, eventually cured by expensive treatment. If the story of his poor background was true, how had his family raised the money? This was one of many questions about Victor Grayson that were never answered.

When he arrived in the House of Commons, he startled many MPs with his uncompromising socialism and silver-tongued championship of those whose lives were stained by poverty. He was the first of the Labour Party's charismatic figures. His speeches spellbound thousands and he was dubbed England's 'finest mob orator.' But he fell foul of Parliamentary rules of behaviour, alienating the more faint-hearted members of the fledgling Party. In the General Election of 1910 he lost his seat and was finished as a politician before he was thirty. From now on he eked out a fairly miserable living as a radical journalist and occasional public speaker. In an article in the left-wing journal *Clarion* in 1911, Grayson became the first person to propose forming a British Socialist Party: 'If we miss this moment, we have missed the opportunity of a century.' A week later he was writing that the BSP was a virtual reality. A serious illness in 1913 kept him away from the political fray, ending the prospect of the foundation of a united Socialist Party. One commentator considered Grayson's was 'a story of buried talents and wasted opportunities'.

His wife Ruth was an actress and a member of a Shakespearean company which, in 1915, was invited to perform in New Zealand. Grayson sailed with her, taking the opportunity, on his arrival, to give antipodean audiences a taste of his blazing oratory. The following year, he enlisted in the New Zealand Army. Towards the end of the war, Ruth died in childbirth – an event that was said to have had a considerable and perhaps permanent effect on Grayson, who now started mixing with people of a different political persuasion, like Horatio Bottomley, the magazine owner and fraudster.

By 1920 he was back in England visiting his mother, still in Liverpool. He finally walked out of the house, telling her he had a speaking engagement in Hull. He left behind a pipe and tobacco and a few photographs, but no clues about his future plans. His mother never saw him again.

One story goes that, instead of travelling to Hull, he went to London, where he joined a group of New Zealand officers for drinks in the Georgian Hotel, off the Strand. A message came for him, delivered, according to one account, by a beautiful woman. Grayson left, saying he would return in a few minutes to finish his whisky, but never came back. A war disability pension piled up in his absence, but he never turned up to collect it. Scotland Yard became involved in the search for the missing politician and it was suggested that his new political friends might have had some connection with his disappearance. It was pointed out that, immediately before the war, he had been living in straitened circumstances, but that afterwards, his lifestyle was luxurious. Was he in the pay of the secret service, some asked. Doubt was even cast on the story that he was a Liverpool carpenter's son.

Over the years several people reported seeing Grayson or hearing his voice. There were alleged sightings at a political meeting in Maidstone in 1924, in Paris in 1934, in Australia where he was allegedly working as a clerk, on top of a bus at Charing Cross, and on a Tube train at Sloane Square station in 1929. His daughter, five when she last saw him in 1919, lived for nearly forty years in the hope that one day the man who had lavished gifts on her would reappear. Not until 1956, when he would have been seventy-five, did she concede that he was probably dead.

In 1975, Sidney Campion, a former Parliamentary reporter who had known Grayson, fuelled speculation when he claimed that, on the eve of the Second World War he was travelling by Tube to the House of Commons when he saw the missing man enter the same compartment wearing a grey suit and (bizarrely for the period) a grey topper. As the train stopped at Westminster, the ex-MP, said Campion, turned to a woman companion and said: 'There's the old talking shop.' Campion got off, but Grayson and the woman stayed on the train, bound for Mansion House. But if Campion was so convinced of the man's identity, why, with his journalistic instincts, did he not challenge the fellow?

One rumour was that Grayson lived in New Zealand for twenty years after his disappearance. Another was that he had been killed in a Chelsea air raid. This provoked a letter from a *Daily Telegraph* reader, asking how anyone could possibly know if the second story was true. The letter was signed by Victor Grayson, the notorious politician's great-nephew.

THE FACELESS MAN

At one o'clock in the morning of a March day in 1982, coal-miner Stephen Dimbleby began his night-shift at Rotherham's Silverwood Colliery. Some 1,000 metres underground, he trudged towards a fourteen-foot-wide tunnel, with his 'snap' bag containing sandwiches and water-bottle slung over his shoulder. All was silent except for the crunch of his boots on the rocky floor. The only light was from his helmet lamp.

Eventually Dimbleby reached an arch of fishplate girders supporting the tunnel roof. Two colleagues had already passed through and were vanishing into the distance, leaving Dimbleby alone. Suddenly, beneath the centre of the arch, another miner's figure appeared. He had not stepped out of the shadows at the side of the tunnel. There was only one way to describe his appearance. He had simply materialised.

In the underground gloom, Dimbleby at first thought he could have been mistaken. Then he noticed something odd about the other man. He was carrying the sort of miner's lamp that had not been used for decades, and on his head an out-of-date safety helmet. That wasn't all. Instead of the orange overalls miners had been wearing for several years, he was dressed in a dusty waistcoat, a collarless shirt and baggy trousers. Now he inclined his head as if acknowledging Dimbleby's presence. It was at this moment that Dimbleby saw something in the glow of the stranger's lamp that made him cry out in horror. The face of the figure before him had no features: no eyes, no nose, no mouth. It was black, but not with streaks of dust. This was the blackness of empty space. Yet the figure seemed to have human substance, with none of the filmy transparency of fictional ghosts. Dimbleby felt that if he reached out, he would touch real flesh and bone. He was not, however, prepared to do so. Instead, he dropped his bag, turned and ran, heading for the spot where he knew he would find his colleagues. His screams echoed mockingly as he stumbled and scrambled over the rocky surface, and somehow managed to turn at speed around each bend of the twisting passage. Colleagues later said it was a miracle that he was able to cover the mile-long distance so quickly. Now they gripped his shoulders and guided him to the pit-cage. As they rose, his body shook. A nurse in the pit medical centre advised treatment for severe shock. In a hospital bed he was later sedated before being driven home.

Vowing he would never go down the pit again, he switched, at his own request, to a surface job, accepting the large wage reduction as inevitable. And the explanation for the visitation? His workmates recalled the tragic death of a miner in a digging-machine in 1968. His restless spirit, they claimed, now haunted the Silverwood mine.

HERE LIES ROBIN (OR DOES HE?)

There are two mysteries about Robin Hood: whether he ever existed and whether he is buried in Yorkshire. Supporters of both propositions aver that he lies in a grave at Kirklees Priory, Cooper's Bridge, Huddersfield, where he met his death at the hands of a vengeful nun. According to an ancient manuscript, he visited the prioress of Kirklees, who some claim was his aunt and who was skilled in medicine, when he was suffering from various ailments including pains in his limbs and a blood affliction. Considering him a foe of all religious persons, she let him bleed to death. After shooting his last arrow, he was buried where it landed under 'a great stone' some 650 yards from the gatehouse. Most historians dismiss his epitaph as spurious and not older than the early eighteenth century. In recent years the tomb has been haunted by members of vampire societies researching what they presume to be an unsolved case of medieval vampirism. Some Hood aficionados even assert he was a native of the West Riding, originally dwelling in what is now Wakefield's shopping centre. What of the legend that links him with Sherwood Forest in Nottinghamshire? The pat answer is that, in his day, huge swathes of Yorkshire woodland stretched as far as the Sherwood region, so that a fugitive from the law might well have travelled this long distance to evade capture.

❄ ❄ ❄

A CLOSE ENCOUNTER?

On a June day in 1980, Zygmunt Adamski, a fifty-seven-year-old Polish-born coal-miner and loving family man, slipped out of his Leeds home to buy potatoes for dinner. It was broad daylight. Five days later his body was found in Todmorden, thirty miles away. He had died of a heart attack. But on his head and neck were burns inflicted two days before the estimated time of his death. Police revealed other bizarre circumstances. Adamski's body was discovered lying atop a pile of coal six feet above the ground. Yet there were no footmarks suggesting anyone had climbed the heap. Moreover, Adamski was spotlessly clean, as if, according to an officer, 'he had stepped from a shower.' Although the site was near a busy railway line, no one had reported seeing anything odd during the hours of Adamski's disappearance. At the inquest, doctors agreed that Adamski's heart attack could have been caused by fright, and his widow expressed the opinion that he had been kidnapped and tortured. The strangest explanation, however, came from ufologists who said that huge orange balls had been seen over Todmorden the week Adamski died. Aliens, they claimed, had scared him, a view that intensified when they heard subsequent reports of another UFO allegedly seen by a policeman who claimed he had been abducted by an alien named Joseph and eight lamp-headed robots, who medically examined him before letting him go. The theory that Adamski had been dropped from the sky, it was argued, was as likely as any other. This was dubbed Yorkshire's mystery of the century.

CHAPTER 6

PERSONS OF NOTE

IMMORTALITY AND MR MARVELL'S HOUSEKEEPER

When Andrew Marvell, the seventeenth-century Hull poet, satirist and politician, died, his housekeeper, Mary Palmer, claimed to be his widow. To this day no one is sure whether or not she was lying. On the one hand, Marvell had no children; on the other, Mary was not only one of his executors but the first person to publish his poems (three years after his death), after finding the manuscript among his effects.

In his lifetime Marvell had never gone with the flow. Sent to Cambridge for his education, he absconded and made his way to London. There his father tracked him down not to some den of booze and dissolution but to a bookshop. He persuaded the youth to return to college.

One of Andrew's later friends was the poet John Milton, who held the official post of Latin secretary to the council of state. By now totally blind, Milton recommended that Marvell be appointed as his assistant. It would be hard, Milton wrote to the council, 'to find a man so fit in every way for that purpose as this gentleman.' It wasn't all that hard. The council gave the job to someone else. Four years later, however, Marvell was more successful and gained the prestigious post. In 1659 he was elected MP for Hull, an office he was to perform skilfully for nineteen years until his death. He wrote satires on Charles II and his court, and, during the monarch's reign, significantly absented himself at one stage from his Parliamentary

Andrew Marvell

duties. He would be better off, he wrote, seeking 'honest fair employment' in Ireland, but this plan came to nothing.

As an MP he took part in debates so rarely that, at the close of one speech, he pointed out that he was not used to this sort of thing and apologised for any unintentional abruptness. Despite his reserved nature, a motion was once passed that he be sent to the Tower for striking another Member and disputing the Speaker's authority. There proved to be so little foundation for these charges that the motion was dropped.

Nonetheless, he became convinced that England was misgoverned, the cause being the King's character: 'for one man's weakness a whole nation bleeds.' He preached the virtues of republicanism and his political satires were so outspoken they had to be published in secret. When the King surprisingly sent an official, the Lord Treasurer, to Marvell's lodgings to ask how he might serve the poet, the poet reportedly replied 'in his usual facetious manner, that it was not in His Majesty's power to serve him'. When, during the same conversation, he was offered a place at court, he still refused. He could not honourably accept, he said, since, should he do so, he would either be 'ungrateful to the King in voting against him, or false to his country in giving in to the measures of the court'. The Lord Treasurer then told Marvell that the King 'had ordered a thousand pounds for him, which he hoped he would receive till he could think what further to ask of His Majesty'. Marvell refused this offer too, though as soon as the Lord Treasurer left, the poet was forced to ask a friend to lend him a guinea. Another version of this story has Marvell summoning his servant, in the Lord Treasurer's presence, and asking the menial: 'Pray, what had I for dinner yesterday?' The servant replied, 'A shoulder of mutton.' 'And what do you allow me today?' 'The remainder hashed.' Exit the Lord Treasurer, now certain that it would be impossible to tempt a fellow of such Spartan habits.

Marvell's sudden death at the age of fifty-seven led to a rumour that political enemies had poisoned him. The suspicion, however, was groundless. It turned out that he had died of a fever 'through the ignorance of an old conceited doctor'. An ounce of

Peruvian bark, it was said, would have saved him, but instead he was given an opiate and copiously bled.

The best description of Marvell was given by the writer John Aubrey, and seems to be a portrait of a man who was a loner by choice: 'He was of a middling stature, pretty strong-set, roundish-faced, cherry-cheeked, hazel eyes, brown hair. He was in his conversation very modest and of very few words. Though he loved wine he would never drink hard in company . . . He kept bottles of wine at his lodging, and many times he would drink liberally by himself to refresh his spirit and exalt his muse.' That muse was responsible for such immortal lines as these:

> But at my back I always hear
> Time's winged chariot hurrying near.
> And yonder all before us lie
> Deserts of vast eternity . . .
> The grave's a fine and private place
> But none I think do there embrace.

It is a disconcerting thought that, but for his housekeeper (or was she really his wife?) such thoughts as these would never have graced literature and entranced the world.

❄ ❄ ❄

WILLIAM AND THE WORM

The acornworm is an odd creature. It takes its name from its front end, shaped like an acorn. This consists of a sucking organ and a collar which it may use to dig into soft sand or mud. It can be up to six feet long and lives in burrows along seashores and in deep water. Its food passes into its mouth and out through gill slits. William Bateson was fascinated by the worm, of which little was known when he began his studies. His interest was to make scientific history. Bateson, born in Whitby in 1861, was to become father of the modern science of genetics. He even invented the word.

The elder son of the Master of St John's College, Cambridge, Bateson was educated at Rugby, which he disliked intensely. Not until he began to study at his father's College did he begin to find himself and decide that natural science was his forte. It was here that he started studying the peculiar acornworm. He worked on the experimental breeding of animals and plants, proving that certain features were inherited, thanks to the presence of genes. In 1908 he became Cambridge University's first professor of genetics and later set up a London centre for genetics research, infecting younger biologists with his enthusiasm.

His sister Mary, born at Robin Hood's Bay, became a respected historian.

❉ ❉ ❉

THE RELUCTANT WHISTLE-BLOWER

His name was Alfred Blunt, and, inevitably, it was said that he was blunt by nature. When a retired Bradford lawyer wrote his biography he called it, wisely, *Blunt,* leaving the reader to make his own inference. Because of one undoubtedly blunt paragraph in a speech delivered to an otherwise tedious conference, he became the most notorious Bishop of Bradford of the twentieth century. The repercussions of his remarks are raked over regularly by the media more than half a century after his death.

Blunt was born in France, where his parents were on holiday, in 1879. His father was an important British official in the Seychelles. Alfred was ordained at twenty-five and, after the 1926 General Strike, joined the Labour Party. Four years later he was offered the Bishopric of Worcester. Two days after accepting, he announced that he refused to live in the castle that was to have been his seat, and would, in fact, sell the old place. Three weeks later, after visiting the castle, he had a change of heart, and decided to live there for a short experimental period. Within three days, however, he reverted to his original stance. 'My wife's doctor, a neurologist, has absolutely and emphatically forbidden me to take her to an isolated place in the country,' he said. He asked the Prime Minister, Ramsay MacDonald, not to publish the reason for his decision (probably linked to his troubled marriage). MacDonald responded by offering him the Bradford incumbency. But before Blunt could be enthroned, he had a nervous breakdown, attributed to years of overwork. He went to Sussex to convalesce, but became so depressed that he felt he must give up the bishopric. The Archbishop of Canterbury, William Temple, would have none of it, and Blunt was consecrated at York Minister on 25

July 1931. He then set off for a month's cruise around the Greek islands, and made yet another unsuccessful attempt to resign.

Despite these inner tensions, Dr Blunt gave the appearance of a congenial and even jolly man. He was portly, with a knowing smile that suggested inner secrets. He smoked a pipe and made all his visitors feel at ease. A Bradford reporter who knew him well once suggested that he would not have batted an eyelid if he had been addressed as 'Alf'. As early as 1933, when the Nazis took power, he was protesting about their treatment of the Jews. A voracious reader, he was said to have ploughed through Jane Austen's novels thirty times, and wrote twenty-five religious books himself. Even more impressively, he could solve *The Times* crossword in half an hour. He was a pastor to the acting profession and produced a

Caricature of Dr Alfred Blunt in the Bradford 'Telegraph & Argus' 4 Dec, 1940

(Courtesy of *The Telegraph & Argus*, Bradford)

string of quotable aphorisms. He objected, for instance, to the singing in church of the 'love lyrics of the stage and the drawing-room'. School examinations, he said, were 'competitions in low cunning between examiners and examinees'. Russian Communism was 'the punishment of God for the iniquities of capitalism'. All children should be taken to church, 'even if they fidget'. And, surprisingly, he saw the opening of cinemas on Sundays as a good thing if they kept young people off the streets. He never feared going out on a limb. 'Human society', he wrote, 'is organised in wrong principles; its guiding motives are self-seeking individualism and the dominance of money.'

On 1 November 1936, he was scheduled to attend a diocesan conference. Despite the Bishop's quotability, Ronald Harker, a young reporter on the Bradford *Telegraph & Argus* (affectionately known as the *T & A*) was less than enthusiastic when he was asked to cover it. As he admitted later when he was a star writer on *The Observer*, he climbed the hill to Church House reluctantly. If he had fallen asleep during the conference, he would have missed the scoop of the century.

This was the year in which the new King, Edward VIII, was involved in a liaison with Mrs Wallis Simpson, a twice-divorced American social climber whose handshake gave her non-admirers the shivers. Although the story of the King's dalliance was well known across the Atlantic, it had achieved no more than the status of a rumour in Britain. American newspapers and magazines that carried stories on the affair were dutifully cut to pieces at the ports of entry. British newspapermen knew what was happening, but, in the forelock-tugging atmosphere of the day, divulged nothing to their readers.

Dr Blunt was disturbed by the party-loving King's casual attitude towards religion. This – and only this, he always claimed – lay behind his dramatic conference pronouncement:

> The benefit of the King's Coronation depends, under God, upon two elements: firstly on the faith, prayer and self-dedication of the King himself; and on that it would be improper for me to say anything except to commend him and ask you to commend him to God's

grace, which he will so abundantly need, as we all need it – for the King is a man like ourselves – if he is to do his duty faithfully. We hope that he is aware of his need. Some of us wish that he gave more positive signs of such awareness.

When Ronald Harker got back to his office, he made directly for the editor's cubicle. He clutched his notebook, from which he read the crucial details of Blunt's speech. The editor, Oliffe Stokes, asked if Harker was sure he had heard aright. Could he stand by his shorthand note? Harker gave the assurance and the story was duly splashed. The Simpson affair was now out in the open.

On 2 December, a *T&A* leader analysed the relevant passage: 'A wide variety of meanings may lurk beneath this remark and many will probably feel that, lacking any degree of direct criticism, it had been better if it had never been expressed.' Others, on the other hand, would consider, the leader continued, that Dr Blunt would not have committed himself in this manner, had he not been convinced that the King's behaviour would make a mockery of the sacramental nature of the planned Coronation ceremony. A columnist in the same paper wrote: 'The Bishop is a first-class speaker without notes, and in transcription a reporter can rarely find any sign of redundancy, or any non-essential phrase; but yesterday he read his speech from a typewritten manuscript and made no departure from the text of it. There was no opportunity either to gauge the reactions of his listeners, for his address had no interruption, and afterwards there was no discussion.' In Leeds the *Yorkshire Post* referred to George V's splendid behaviour as a monarch: 'Deep disappointment must necessarily result if, instead of this continuity of example, there should develop a dispute between the King and his Ministers such as must almost inevitably raise a constitutional issue of the gravest character.' The Press Association flashed these words to every newspaper in the land.

Unless he was being disingenuous, Blunt expressed mortification at the interpretation of his remarks. In private notes he wrote:

For one moment I appeared in the pages of history and became front page news in *The Times*; my part in the events leading up to King

Edward VIII's Abdication has been absurdly exaggerated, and so completely misrepresented by the gossip columns of the Press and the current scandal-mongering of gutters and clubs alike, and I think it may be of interest if I set down what actions I had to do with the events. We (the Church) were all trying to key England up to approach the Coronation with some sense of religious education.

Blunt referred to another leading churchman's report of a businessman's remark. 'You parsons are trying to make us take a religious view of the Coronation. What's the use when the principal actor in it has no use for that sort of thing himself?' He had planned his speech, he said, to deal with this very point:

Note the words, for they were carefully chosen. I did not deny that the King showed signs of grace. Indeed I thought – and think – the exact reverse, for much of his quality was too good to be due to anything but God's grace. Nor did I say that the King was not aware that he needed the grace of God; that was his own business and I had neither right nor knowledge to speak about it. But I did know that, so far as public acknowledgement of God in religious observance was concerned, the King had gone a different way from his father. Nobody could know that he valued the public observance of religion and I believed that to be a real weakness in his public attitude as King of England. My words referred to this and this alone. I wrote my address in October and had it typed by my secretary, and put it aside for use in December when the Conference was to meet. At that time, I had never heard of Mrs Simpson and knew nothing whatever of the King's 'affair' with her.

In the *Diocesan News* of January, 1937, Blunt said: 'The press revelation ended a period of silence and underground gossip, but in itself it made no difference to the outcome.'

The final comment came from the Duke of Windsor, who, in his memoirs, described Blunt's speech as 'the spark that caused the explosion'.

DEMOCRAT IN A DOG-COLLAR

The Revd Geoffrey Studdert-Kennedy is a bit of a mouthful. He was more affectionately known as Woodbine Willie, for his habit of distributing cigarettes to the troops as a First World War chaplain.

A clergyman's son, Studdert-Kennedy was born in St Mary's vicarage, Quarry Hill, Leeds. For a time he served as a curate under his father. He was frail and asthmatic (a condition, perhaps, caused by personal indulgence in Woodbines?). When he left a slum parish in Rugby in 1916 he become possibly the best-known padre on the Western Front. In 1917 he won the MC at Messines, and Tommies showed a lively appreciation of his inspirational talks at the base camps through which they passed. One talk, titled 'Christ or the Kaiser', delivered during Lent at Rouen to a packed audience of officers and men, was cheered to the echo. His versified meditations, *Rough Rhymes of a Padre* (1918), originally printed in thousands of pocket editions, became a best-seller even after the war.

The terrible conflict, however, turned Studdert-Kennedy into a pacifist, causing a radical redirection of his life. Though he was no intellectual, the themes of his post-war speeches to mass audiences, including pit-head miners, drew much from the early social thinking of his friend William Temple, the future Archbishop of Canterbury. He became a convert to what was described as Christian Socialism, advancing an idealistic vision of society bonded by service and co-operation under a disinterested and rational leadership. Some might call him a foolhardy optimist.

Other books he wrote became best-sellers in cheap editions and were serialised in local newspapers around the country: *The Hardest Part* (1918), *Lies* (1919), *Democracy and the Dog-Collar* (1921),

Woodbine Willie

(Courtesy of *History Today*)

Food for the Fed Up (1921), *The Wicket Gate* (1923) and *The Word and the Work* (1925). Throughout the 1920s he articulated his concerns about the class war, public greed and threats to the unity achieved during the war. Despite his left-wing aspirations, he dismissed Karl Marx as an enemy of individual personality and a prophet of regimentation, and he became a welcome speaker at TUC conferences. At a particularly successful overflow meeting, one paper reported, 'women wept and men broke down.'

In 1986 a new chapel at Leeds Parish Church was dedicated to Woodbine Willie's memory. It included a tapestried altarpiece with a dove of peace as the main motif, and Flanders poppies in the background.

An odd footnote: in the Second World War, a British tank in the North African campaign was named Woodbine Lizzie, after one Alice Parker, believed to be a Leeds doctor's wife, who, after separating from him, became that rarity, a female tramp, wearing several layers of heavy clothes and a tram-driver's cap. On one wintry day she was seen stripped to the waist washing herself in a fountain. She smoked incessantly, asking passers-by if they could spare a Woodbine.

❄ ❄ ❄

THE MASKED PROFESSOR

There must have been times when, in his old age, the tall, white-haired Adam Sedgwick seemed a scary figure. To relieve a bronchial condition, he would often be seen wearing a respirator. In fact, this pioneering geologist was loved by many of his contemporaries, and, after his death, respected by both scientists and historians. In 1985, in the Dales village of Dent, where he was born, there was even a festival in his honour.

Sedgwick is mainly remembered for his identification of early palaeozoic strata, his friendship with Queen Victoria, and his spat with a former student, Charles Darwin, whose fame was to out-live his own.

A parson's son, Sedgwick was born in 1785, delivered by his father's one-time maths tutor, then practising as a surgeon. Sedgwick was to describe his home with his parents, three brothers and three sisters, as humble. 'But', he wrote, 'we were a motley crew, rich in health and rich in brotherly love.'

As a boy, he attended the local school, where his godfather was teacher. Initially, he found that ripping books to pieces was more pleasurable than reading them. Known to villagers as Adam o' th' Parson's, he was often entrusted with important errands. Strong and energetic, he would explore the local countryside, a habit that instilled in him the observational powers that were to mark his career.

Even as a child he displayed curiosity about engineering techniques, especially the construction of the tower at Dent Church, an event whose technical details he still remembered eighty-three years later.

In 1818 he became a geology professor at Cambridge, but would make frequent visits to Dent, where he befriended an old soldier down on his luck. On each visit, he would present the veteran with a plug of tobacco. When the old man was removed to a workhouse, he asked Sedgwick, noted for his kindness, to exchange the baccy for a small daily glass of grog.

Though Sedgwick's best-known researches took place in the Lake District and North Wales, he devoted a year to the chalk wolds and cliffs from Holderness to Whitby, 'a dirty stinking town in a very picturesque situation'. He was a strong believer in following the customs of the territory he was covering, and on a Highland geological trip made several stops along the way to eat haggis, sup whisky and dance in hobnailed boots.

His students found him a hard man to keep up with. Some fifty of them would gallop on horseback to chosen locations, where he would describe interesting geological features, and he would think nothing of covering fifty miles a day.

When former student Charles Darwin sent him a copy of his *The Origin of Species*, Sedgwick replied that he had read the book 'with more pain than pleasure', adding, 'Parts of it I admired greatly, parts I laughed at till my sides were almost sore; other parts I read with absolute sorrow, because I think them utterly false and mischievous.' He compared Darwin's ideas to an eccentric contemporary's plan for a locomotive that would sail to the moon.

When Prince Albert became Chancellor of Cambridge University (where Sedgwick later founded an eponymous museum), the two men developed an admiration for each other, and Queen Victoria invited the professor to Balmoral, where he was amused to see the twenty-eight-year-old monarch blush as she rose to speak to him for the first time. On Albert's death, she sent Sedgwick a memorial lithograph of herself and her late consort. Sedgwick admitted he 'wept like a child'. Eventually, the Queen summoned him to Windsor. 'I believe', he later recalled, 'I was the first person, out of her own family, to whom she fully opened her heart, and told of her sorrows.' Soon afterwards, she sent him a bound copy of Albert's speeches inscribed, 'From his broken-hearted widow, Victoria.'

As an elderly man Sedgwick suffered from gout, vertigo, stomach complaints and the bronchial ailment that drove him to wear a respirator. 'While they try to cure one part of my old, nearly worn-out machinery,' he confided in a letter, 'they damage another. 'Tis something like putting new wine in old bottles, or like the work of a tinker who in patching an old kettle produces two rents in place of the old one.'

Arguably the greatest Victorian geologist, Sedgwick, who died at eighty-eight, is as much remembered for campaigning against slavery and child labour as for being the first man to unearth Britain's earliest fossil-bearing rocks. He is buried in Cambridge, and, after his death, the people of Dent set up a huge slab of grey-pink granite with an inset drinking fountain in the cobbled Main Street, near his father's church.

SUFFER THE LITTLE CHILDREN

In September 1830, an extraordinarily long and vehement letter appeared in the *Leeds Mercury*. Headed 'Yorkshire Slavery', it deplored the appalling conditions endured by children working in Bradford mills. It noted the high-mindedness of those concerned about slavery abroad alongside their indifference to the cruelties on their own doorstep. It was to become one of the century's most famous, indeed sensational letters. Yet its writer was the steward of a country estate, who, until recently, had had little knowledge of industrial life. Over the coming years he was to achieve both fame and notoriety as a fervent campaigner on behalf of those unfortunate children, a Tory but almost a revolutionary. His name was Richard Oastler.

Born in Leeds in 1789, Oastler was, at thirty-one, the £300-a-year steward at Fixby Hall, a large estate near Huddersfield, when he received what was to be the most fateful invitation of his life: to visit a friend, John Wood, a prominent Bradford worsted spinner, reputedly running the largest business of its kind in the country. His prosperity was indicated by his purchase of Horton Hall, a stately mansion standing on a hill at the city's edge. He was a man of some sensibility, given to charitable works, and he was disturbed by the long hours women and children were compelled to work in the mills. Unburdening his concerns to his guest, he told how, even in his own mills, children worked from six in the morning till seven at night all the year round, with only a forty-minute noon break. Other mills, he went on, gave no breaks at all to the children, who had to nibble the food they brought with them at snatched moments while the machines were still running. Even worse, children who arrived late, fell asleep in the late afternoon or were tardy in repairing snapped spindle threads, were mercilessly strapped. Remarkably, their employers were said to be pious men, keen advocates of temperance, overseas missions and the building of chapels.

Oastler was astonished and overwhelmed by a feeling of personal guilt. From his window at Fixby he had watched the building of factories in Huddersfield but had never given them more than a passing thought.

The next morning a valet brought a message that Wood would like to see him before he left. He found his friend reading the Bible by candlelight. 'I have had no sleep tonight,' said Wood. 'I have been reading this book and in every page I have read my own condemnation. I cannot allow you to leave me without a pledge that you will use all your influence in trying to remove from our factory system the cruelties which are practised in our mills.' Oastler promised to do what he could. It was a promise that would change the course of his life and England's social and political history. On his return to Fixby, he wrote his historic letter. It read in part:

> Thousands of our fellow-creatures and fellow-subjects, both male and female, the miserable inhabitants of a *Yorkshire town* . . . are this very moment existing in a state of slavery, *more horrid* than are the victims of that hellish system *'colonial slavery!'* These innocent creatures drawl out, unpitied, their short but miserable existence in a place famed for its profession of religious zeal. The very streets which receive the droppings of an 'Anti-Slavery Society' are every morning wet from the tears of innocent victims at the accursed shrine of avarice, who are *compelled* (not by the cart-whip of the negro slave-driver but by the dread of the equally appalling thong or strap of the over-looker) to hasten half-dressed *but not half-fed* to those magazines of British infantile slavery – the worsted mills in the town and neighbourhood of Bradford!!!

He signed the letter 'A Briton'.

He took it personally to the *Mercury* office, where he handed it to the editor, who, after reading it twice, appeared nonplussed and expressed his surprise at the alleged facts it detailed. Though admitting some scepticism, he agreed to publish the letter above Oastler's name instead of a *nom de plume*. Its eventual appearance marked the start of a seventeen-year campaign for legislation to protect the child mill-workers. The period saw episodes both dramatic and bizarre, and the development of the mild-mannered Oastler into a vigorous orator with a mastery of invective.

The letter itself had such an impact that a Radical bookshop in Leeds had it printed as a broadsheet, which was plastered all over the town and hung in pubs. Oastler's health was toasted at a dinner commemorating the recent French Revolution. His opponents were also quick to respond. One mill master pointed out that little girls were necessary for spinning machines as they were quick and clean, and, though their days were long, their work was 'far from laborious'. By working in the mills, the children also received splendid training, learning regularity and discipline, the virtues of early rising and how to be self-supporting.

Some months later six Huddersfield mill-workers called on Oastler and persuaded him to join them in fighting for industrial reform, putting aside their political and sectarian differences. This became known as the Fixby Hall Compact. One of the six, Joshua Hobson, a self-educated hand-loom weaver, was later to become editor of the *Huddersfield Chronicle*.

Oastler and the men met weekly at the Ship Inn. Known as the Short Time Committee, they also became Oastler's bodyguards. They kept him informed of factory news and workers' gossip, and facts with which to counter the employers' arguments. He became not only an inspiring leader but their personal friend, to the end of their lives.

At one public meeting in Huddersfield, Oastler told a dramatic story of a seven-year-old girl who had recently collapsed and died through the treatment she had received at work: 'If the [factory] bell had ceased to ring when she arrived with trembling, shivering, weary limbs at the factory door, there stood a monster in human form before her and as she passed he lashed her.' At this point Oastler struck the lectern with a long, heavy strap. 'This,' he cried, holding up the strap, 'is no fiction. It was hard at work in this town last week, and I have seen the effects of such inhumanity in black marks from the necks to the seats of children.' Whenever possible, Oastler personally investigated cases of cruelty, and children who had been made ill or deformed through their work were brought to him for help. Some sought leg-irons for withered limbs, others assistance in getting hospital beds. Meanwhile Oastler documented such trickery by employers as manipulating factory clocks to lengthen the working day.

One of the campaign's oustanding events was a pilgrimage to York that presaged the Jarrow March of the 1930s. While peals echoed from the steeple of the old parish church, some 24,000 workers convened in Leeds, whence they advanced on York, with bands playing and flags fluttering and carrying home-made banners. They slept in barns and warehouses on the way, and inns were warned to supply each customer with bread, beer and cheese. Every man was given a food ticket, to be exchanged on the journey. Men who had no shoes borrowed a pair for the march. Others trudged all the way in clogs. Some even wore borrowed coats or woollen blankets.

Oastler had to call on York's High Sheriff to reassure him after persons of ill will claimed the marchers would plunder farms, burn hay-ricks, slaughter flocks and, in a grand climax, sack York. Accusing Oastler of delusions of grandeur, the *Leeds Mercury* said he imagined himself to be a king. The tag immediately caught the workers' fancy, and from now on he was popularly known as The Factory King.

After a five-hour meeting in York, the march back began in pelting rain, and hundreds of worn-out men with blistered and bleeding feet begged shelter in taverns, cottages and sheds. A parson who was one of Oastler's most steadfast supporters hired covered wagons and, with colleagues, drove through the night picking up stragglers and administering restoratives. When Oastler himself finally got into his own bed, the skin of his feet peeled off with his stockings.

The *Mercury* poured scorn on the whole enterprise, and 200 Leeds marchers were so enraged they paraded in the town led by a man carrying the offending copy of the newspaper tied with black crêpe to the top of a pole. Reaching the *Mercury* office, they lit the paper and hissed. Later a procession set forth from the Union Inn carrying an effigy of the editor inscribed, 'The great Liar of the North'. It was then stuck on top of a bonfire outside the *Mercury* office, and, to the catcalls of the mob, burned to ashes.

The battle to persuade Parliament to pass remedial legislation led to the setting up of a Select Committee, which eventually produced a 982-page report that became one of the most famous British state papers of the century. It told of compulsory night-shifts and the sacking of children who refused to turn up. Some hands were kept in a factory for forty-eight hours or more at a stretch, taking their rest on straw or sacking dumped in a corner. Dust and fluff made the workers' food filthy as soon as it was unpacked, and the noon break was often cut short for the cleaning of machines. Rooms stank of machine oil and grease, and, in winter, gas-lamps. The Select Committee heard evidence from deformed children and one overlooker told MPs he had visited 200 families where youngsters were deformed, 'thrown crooked by the practice of . . . throwing up the left shoulder and bending the right knee'. Many witnesses said the children had to be thrashed to keep them awake, and some older girls were seduced by foremen or even masters. Several of the men who gave evidence before the Committee were sacked when they returned to Yorkshire.

After the Select Committee came a Royal Commission. By now Oastler had become so frustrated and distrustful that he had the Commission members shadowed as they went about their investigations. The amateur sleuths noted the places the Commissioners visited, the witnesses they examined, the pressures to which they were subjected, the people they dined with and even the food they ate.

When the three investigators assigned to Yorkshire arrived, as they thought, unobtrusively in Leeds, their presence was soon rumbled. The town was plastered with posters urging the factory children to demonstrate the next evening. Accordingly, as soon as the mills closed, some 3,000 ragged and grimy children gathered in the Free Market, whence they marched to the Commissioner's hotel. The Commissioners received a deputation, following which the crowd outside burst into the Song of the Factory Children, whose lyrics demanded new protective laws.

Meanwhile Oastler's men received reports of the preparations made in the mills the Commissioners were due to visit. Walls were whitewashed, sick children excluded and the rest ordered to come to work in their best clothes. Oastler had an enjoyable time exposing all this skulduggery. He also sent an over-the-top letter to the Commissioners in Yorkshire that began: 'I solemnly protest against your Commission and against your proceedings: in the name of the Father, and of the Son and of the Holy Ghost' and went on to give seventeen examples of their 'un-English behaviour'.

The Commissioners moved on to Bradford, and, at the end of their visit, made an attempt to shake off the men tailing them. Announcing they were now going to Keighley, they had coach tickets made out to this destination. With a horse already saddled, they switched at the last moment for the night coach to Doncaster. Their trackers immediately reported the news and, within a few minutes, a horseman was on their trail.

Oastler's campaign was a saga that only ended in 1847 with the passing of an Act ruling that children aged between nine and eighteen must not work more than ten hours a day, exclusive of meal times.

His career had been marked by a personal disaster. For his opposition to the Poor Law Amendment Act of 1834 (under which indigent farm-hands could be compelled to work in factories for meagre wages), his employer fired him and had him imprisoned for debt. From 1841 to 1843 he was in London's Fleet Prison, where he elaborated his social theories in his three-volume *Fleet Papers*. Afterwards he edited *The Home*, a family magazine addressed primarily to the working classes.

※ ※ ※

ALL TOGETHER NOW

When we hear the raucous chants of football crowds, the man to blame is Eric Godley of Harrogate, who claimed, until his death at eighty-seven in 1963, to have invented the concept of community singing. He once led a crowd singing in the streets outside St Martin-in-the-Fields, London, an experiment that proved so popular it caused traffic jams and had to be called off.

A Knaresborough cobbler's son, Godley originally pursued his father's trade. As a boy chorister at Leeds Parish Church he was trained by a former pupil of Liszt. He also cycled to York for music lessons. While still in his teens he won first prize in the bass section of a contest at Pudsey Mechanics' Institute, the adjudicator advising the audience that they had been listening to one of the world's future great singers. He eventually embarked on a professional career with his wife, a contralto. In 1906 he sang at the Royal Albert Hall. This led to an invitation to sing at a reception for Queen Alexandra, the Kaiser and the Dowager Empress of Russia. After a spell as a Covent Garden opera singer, he was booked for the Berlin Opera, an appointment he never took up because of the outbreak of the First World War.

❊ ❊ ❊

A SONG TO REMEMBER

There was 'Tipperary' and there was 'Keep The Home Fires Burning', but no First World War song was more poignant than 'Roses of Picardy'. It became a melody that never died. Written in 1916 it was recorded so often it crossed into new musical eras. It was chosen by singers as diverse as Al Jolson and Perry Como. During the war itself one artiste who sang it regularly did so with tears streaming down her cheeks.

The words were by a now forgotten lyricist named Fred Weatherly, but his first attempt to find an appropriate tune failed. The music was turned down by a publisher, and another composer, Haydn Wood, only twenty-four years old, was asked to see what he could do. He obliged and the rest is musical history.

Wood was born in Slaithwaite, near Huddersfield, in 1882. The Colne Valley had been a cradle of song ever since large numbers of Welsh people, attracted by the woollen industry, had settled there. Shortly before the birth, the young father-to-be, thrilled by a performance of Franz Joseph Haydn's oratorio, *The Creation*, vowed that if his child turned out to be a boy, he would be named after the Austrian composer. And so he was.

Haydn played the violin as a small child, and, when his family moved to the Isle of Man, audiences there were entranced by his performances. Or, at least, most of them were. When the theatre in which he was playing retained his services, he had hardly raised his bow for the first show of the second week when his mother, in the audience, heard a voice behind her: 'Here's that terrible kid again.'

At fourteen Wood won an open scholarship to the Royal College of Music, where he studied the violin and composition. Here he met a soprano from Liverpool named Dorothy Court.

He was twenty-two when he found himself on a world tour with a leading Canadian opera singer, Emma Albani, whom he accompanied on the fiddle. Albani, who had been a great friend of Queen Victoria, had the disconcerting habit of bending down to tie a shoe-lace while aiming for a bell-like top C. Nonetheless, the pair were fêted everywhere and received by royalty.

Wood, meanwhile, had been composing several works in the classical style, including a quartet for strings which won him a prize, and a piano concerto.

In 1909 he married Dorothy Court, the girl whom he had met at college, and who now had several D'Oyly Carte Opera principal rôles under her belt. She was a great populariser, and persuaded her husband to join her on music-hall tours. In old age he denied her assertion that she 'ruined him for life'. He never regretted the day, he insisted, when he 'met his fate.'

The songs he composed for her brought him fame and wealth and a warm place in the hearts of millions. Apart from 'Roses of Picardy', popular melodies he created included 'A Brown Bird Singing' (words by *Peter Pan* author J.M. Barrie), 'Love's Garden of Roses' and 'Bird of Love Divine'. One of his lyricists was Lilian Glanville, a direct descendant of Lord Byron. She gave the Woods an Easter egg of Bristol blue glass in a silver nest, which had once belonged to the poet.

Wood also wrote *Elizabeth of England* for the Queen's

Coronation, a Yorkshire suite for piano, and another suite on Britain's royal castles. One of his pieces, 'The Horse Guards, Whitehall', became the signature tune of the BBC radio series *Down Your Way*. In 1956, he was presented with the Ivor Novello Award for his outstanding contribution to British popular music. In all, he had written more than 200 songs, fifteen suites, nine rhapsodies, three large-scale concertante pieces, and sixty assorted orchestral works. Fittingly, the little Yorkshire mill town in which he was born boasts its own, highly respected symphony orchestra.

❊ ❊ ❊

LIKE FATHER, LIKE SON

A Whitby sculpture of a ship's crow's-nest celebrates the lives of the local Scoresbys, father and son, both seafarers and whaling skippers, who not only charted the Arctic but were scientists and inventors. William Scoresby senior was a twenty-year-old farm worker when he signed on as an apprentice to the captain of the *Jane*, a ship trading from Whitby to the Baltic. He had already studied navigation, and, in only his second year at sea, detected a reckoning error that might have caused the ship's loss. His only reward was the ill will of the first mate, whose blunder he had exposed. This led him to leave the ship and transfer to an ordnance vessel, the *Speedwell*, carrying supplies to Gibraltar. At the entrance to the Straits, she was captured by the Spanish fleet. He was incarcerated in a Spanish jail, but escaped to Cadiz, where he boarded an English vessel that took him home, where he resumed farm work. In 1785, however, the lure of the sea proved irresistible and he joined a whaler, the *Henrietta*, sailing on her for six years and visiting Greenland each summer. When the captain retired, Scoresby took over. His next vessel, the *Dundee*, was an unlucky choice. She was trapped in ice for two months. In 1802 he joined a small Whitby company and became part-owner of a new trading ship, the *Resolution*, which he commanded for six years. In 1806 he forced her through a formidable icefield to come within 510 miles of the North Pole, the northernmost point then reached by any sailing ship. After the voyage of 1810, he resigned the command in favour of his son, William junior, he himself taking over the *John*, another whaler. This post too he eventually relinquished, this time in his son-in-law's favour. When his next ship was destroyed by fire in the Orkneys, he retired to Whitby. In all, he had made thirty voyages and invented an ice drill and the crow's nest, in which he would sometimes spend innumerable hours. It provided protection for men on the look-out for whales, icebergs or channels through treacherous ice, and was described as 'the greatest boon of modern times ever given to the Arctic navigator.'

Postcard depicting sculpture of William Scoresby's Crow's Nest

William Scoresby junior first sailed at the age of ten. The vessel was a whaler, the destination Greenland and the skipper his father. On his return he was sent back to school, joining the *Resolution* at fourteen. Year after year he made the Greenland voyage with his father, until 1806 when he enrolled at Edinburgh University, where he studied chemistry and natural philosophy. When, after finishing his course, he was put in command of a gunboat, he complained to an admiral that she was not seaworthy. His warning was ignored, and the vessel had scarcely reached open sea when she began taking in water and had to be abandoned. Scoresby and the crew boarded another vessel that hove alongside. He then tried a seaman's life in the Navy at a time when lashings were commonplace. Studying the natural history of the polar region, he made a series of revolutionary drawings of snowflakes as seen through a microscope, and collected many specimens of then unknown plants. He invented an instrument called a marine diver for obtaining deep-sea temperatures, and created fire with a lens fashioned from ice. In 1819 his scientific work led to his election as a Fellow of the Royal Society of Edinburgh, and his two-volume work on the Arctic was later regarded as seminal.

When the younger Scoresby's wife died, he turned to religion, studied for the ministry and was eventually ordained to a curacy at Bessingby, near Bridlington, at a twentieth of his seagoing salary. In 1827 he became chaplain to a Liverpool sailors' church, and, later, vicar of Bradford, only resigning when his health failed. In 1851, in a splendidly filial gesture, he published *My Father, being Records of the Adventurous Life of the late W. Scoresby.*

❄ ❄ ❄

MARY'S MISSION

Established in 1686, the Bar Convent in York was the first girls' school in England. Though it has now ceased to function as a traditional school, it has taken on a different educational rôle: that of public museum and associated youth centre. Its founder, Mother Frances Bedingfield, was the companion of one of the least-known but most remarkable figures in religious history, Mary Ward, a pioneer of women's education. Mary herself founded the first unenclosed order for women, and, after her death, her congregation set up the York school.

Born into a Catholic household at Mulwith, near Boroughbridge, in 1585, Mary grew up in a society antagonistic towards her faith. During her childhood, her father's library boasted a special hidey-hole behind a secret panel for priests on the run from their persecutors. Little Mary herself would save her pennies to help Catholics languishing in prison because of their beliefs. She even gave two hens that had been her special pets. Generosity and humility became the themes of her life. As a guest in a mansion, she typically made a point of donning a maid's apron and cleaning the lobby with a cloth and bucket of water.

Attitudes towards the Catholics eventually led her to leave the country in the year of the Gunpowder Plot, most of whose conspirators were her relatives. She opened a string of religious schools around Europe. In the French town of St Omer, with a large basket on her arm, Mary begged food in the streets for a local convent. After opening her first Continental school in St Omer, she travelled on foot wearing a pilgrim's outfit of cloak, high beaver hat, staff and cast-off shoes. As she and her followers did not lead cloistered lives or wear nuns' habits, they irritated many Catholics, who spied on them. Men unconcerned with religious niceties found dark-eyed Mary attractive and one rich nobleman sent his footmen to her lodgings with gifts of sweets and preserved fruits. After sending them back she bolted herself in her room.

In her schools Mary and her devotees practised asceticism, eating only once a day and sleeping on straw beds. An unimpressed Archbishop of Canterbury reportedly said: 'That woman has done more harm than many priests.'

In 1617 she was back home with fresh members for her growing Yorkshire community. Hearing that the hostile Archbishop wished to see her, she decided to call on him at Lambeth Palace. With two colleagues in bright taffeta gowns and stylish ruffs, she entered the Archbishop's study. When a footman stiffly advised the ladies that the prelate was not at home, Mary slipped a diamond ring from her finger and scratched her name on a window-pane, her version of a calling card.

Those who had spied on Mary eventually closed in on her, and arrested her. She appeared before judges at London's Guildhall, and though aware that possession of a rosary was an offence punishable by loss of property or life imprisonment, drew hers from her pocket and wound it round her fingers. When an apoplectic judge swore, Mary reproved him. In her blunt Yorkshire manner, she called him 'a miserable man, a good-for-nothing wretch'. She was at once dragged to a cell, where she knelt and kissed the threshold, so impressing her guards that they treated her with considerable deference. She was sentenced to death, but, fearing the odium they might incur by going ahead with the execution, the authorities released her and allowed her to cross the Channel once more.

When she opened one of her free schools in Rome, the citizenry were delighted at the prospect of having their children kept out of mischief all day, with no fees to pay. At first they had looked askance at Mary's staff in their black dresses, white wimples, white bands across their foreheads and white cuffs, who did not live, like orthodox nuns, behind grilles. But soon parents, priests and august cardinals alike were won over. Only the Roman underworld expressed concern. If such refined schools for girls were allowed to stay in business, they argued, there was no future at all for the city's bordellos.

Mary died aged sixty at Heworth, near York, and was interred in the only available burial ground, the Protestant churchyard at Osbaldwick. Her body was removed, probably during Oliver Cromwell's régime, but by whom nobody knows. Her schools were to become the models for modern Catholic women's religious institutes.

✳ ✳ ✳

THE MAN WHO HATED BEING SEASICK

Without him, Sheffield might never have become the City of Steel. The Great King of Steel, as Sir Henry Bessemer was known, responded to the need for guns during the Crimean War by inventing an economical process that turned molten pig-iron directly into steel by blowing air through it in a tilting converter that was to bear his name. In 1858 he set up a steelworks in Sheffield specialising in guns and, later, steel rails. From then on the city's industrial future was assured.

Bessemer was a prolific inventor. His first, when he was only twenty, was inspired by the £100,000 a year the Government was losing by repeated, fraudulent use of stamps affixed to deeds. He made this impossible by creating perforated dies, so that a date could be indelibly impressed on every stamp. He learned the ancient Oriental art of manufacturing gold paint, and invented a steam-driven press to extract juice from sugar cane.

He did, however, experience one enormous failure, an attempt to build a ship's saloon cabin in which passengers would not become seasick.

Bessemer had a personal interest. He suffered from *mal de mer* himself. After one particularly nauseous episode, his doctor administered small doses of prussic acid, which he thankfully survived. He now felt that the problem could be averted if the passenger section could be isolated so far from the rest of the ship that it would neither roll nor pitch.

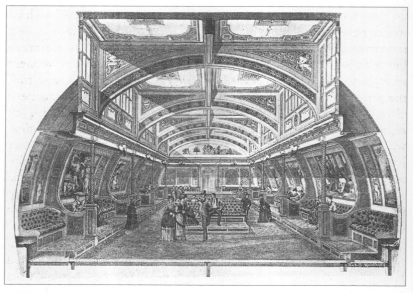

Interior view of the anti-seasickness saloon

His complex concept involved a suspended cabin (also known as a swinging saloon) in which the ship's motion would be controlled by hydraulic power. The cabin would be circular, with seats all around its circumference, and a gallery above, also with seats. The floor would be large enough to serve as a promenade, and below the floor a heavy weight would hang to keep it horizontal. He admitted his idea was, to some extent, crude, but after making a table-top model in which a clockwork mechanism kept the tiny ship pitching, he graduated to the real thing, despite the insomnia and headaches the project was causing. From a Hull shipyard he ordered a vessel that would incorporate his saloon. The job was duly done, and the saloon itself was a luxurious affair, with oak carvings, paintings, gilt decorations, morocco-covered seats and spiral columns. Some hailed it as the greatest wonder of its kind since the Hanging Gardens of Babylon.

The ship was named the *Bessemer* and a trial of the vessel and its anti-nausea saloon was advertised for 8 May 1875. Three weeks before then, however, it was decided that there should be a rehearsal. In mid-April, the boat set off from Dover for Calais in beautifully calm weather. Unfortunately, the captain failed to steer safely into the French harbour and crashed the paddle wheels into the pier. By this point the machinery in the saloon itself had been almost but not totally completed. The next three weeks were spent repairing the paddle wheels in time for the public trial. No time was left for completion work on the saloon machinery. Bessemer had the saloon riveted to the main ribs and bottom of the ship, and on the second trip the passengers were impressed by the saloon's décor. They were less impressed when, yet again, the ship smashed into the Calais pier, knocking its huge timbers down 'like so many ninepins'. As Bessemer's hydraulic controlling apparatus had not been completed, he felt that it had not, in effect, been tested at sea, and that, consequently, nobody could claim that it had failed. The double catastrophe, however, Bessemer wrote in his autobiography, 'deprived me of one of the greatest triumphs of a long, professional life'. He went on 'I had fondly hoped to remove for ever from thousands yet unborn the bitter pangs of the Channel passage and thus . . . to strengthen the bonds of mutual respect and esteem between two great nations . . . All this had gone for ever.'

His Bessemer Saloon Steamboat Company was wound up, though Bessemer himself repeated that its collapse 'was not caused by any failure of my invention, which remains to this hour an untried mechanical problem'.

A failure, however, it was, and the Hull shipyard went back to the construction of more orthodox vessels, while people continued to be seasick.

❋ ❋ ❋

ANCIENT PLUTOCRAT

After fighting for William the Conqueror at the Battle of Hastings, William of Warenne, a Norman lord, was rewarded with the grant of lands that included the vast manor of Wakefield, which then stretched from Normanton to Todmorden. He amassed land in eighteen counties in all and is now believed to have been the richest Briton, albeit an immigrant, of the last millennium. Today, it has been estimated, he would be worth £57 billion, putting Bill Gates, the American computer supremo, in the shade. By his death in 1088 his assets are thought to have been worth 6.66 per cent of the net national income. His family was responsible for the erection of Sandal Castle, Wakefield, which was used as a defensive enclosure (now in ruins). The Warenne line was diluted through marriage to the Arundel and Norfolk families, and the remains of his fortune can be traced to the present Earl of Arundel.

❋ ❋ ❋

THE GINGERBREAD BOY

The father of William Etty, the York-born painter, specialised in gingerbread, on which the young William no doubt doted. 'My first panels on which I drew', William wrote in a short autobiography, 'were the boards of my father's shop-floor; my first crayon a farthing's worth of white chalk, but my pleasure amounted to ecstasy when my mother promised me next morning, if I were a good boy, I should use some colours, mixed with gum-waters. I was so pleased I could scarcely sleep.' In 1798 he started a seven-year apprenticeship to a Hull letterpress printer. In response to William's repeated requests, an uncle invited him to London, where he was free to paint. His friends thought of him as 'a worthy plodding person, with no chance of ever becoming a good painter.' He proved them wrong. During a spell in Venice, where for centuries art had almost been a way of life, the local people reported: 'He paints with the fury of a devil and the sweetness of an angel.' For much of his life he was poor and in debt, but even when he was successful, he attended life classes at the Royal Academy every night like a student. In 1830 he was in Paris, then in the throes of revolution, and found himself 'painting in the Louvre when grapeshot were pouring on the populace . . . and musketry rattled everywhere'. He painted 'not the Draper's or Milliner's Work – but God's more glorious work', in other words, female nudes, which are still greatly admired.

THE FATHER OF FLIGHT

If he were alive today Sir George Cayley would have been termed an Ideas Man. He was positively bursting with them. He came up with countless inventions he did not even bother to patent, leaving others to reap the glory that should rightly have been his.

The squire of Brompton, near Scarborough, Cayley hated hunting, then considered a normal pursuit for gentlemen of his rank. He was happiest in his workshop, and his agricultural methods were supremely beneficial to the farmers of his Vale of Pickering community. By draining boggy ground in the Vale he released thousands of good acres for farming, and in 1825 he invented a caterpillar tractor.

During the Napoleonic scare, he published a conscription plan under which a quarter of all able-bodied men would be called up for twenty days in any year for intensive military training. He founded and commanded a defence volunteer corps (a virtual Dads' Army) in the Scarborough district, though, he later said, 'they were never called upon to sabre more than roast beef or bleed other than in port, drinking loyal toasts.' When twenty-three firemen died in a London theatre blaze, he designed what he considered to be a safer type of theatre, with sheet-iron safety curtains, no doors opening inwards and exits as large as possible. Floors, he said, should slope so that no theatregoer's view was obscured by the person sitting in front, obvious to us now but revolutionary in his day. He offered ideas for guided missiles to the Duke of Wellington, and, when eleven men drowned in a lifeboat disaster off Scarborough, put forward ideas for a lifeboat that, he claimed, would be unsinkable and self-righting in a storm-tossed sea. After a series of railway accidents he concluded that a positive law was needed (again obvious to us today) that 'up' trains should keep to one line, and 'down' trains to another. He spent three years developing plans for a railway from Scarborough to Malton, York and Tadcaster, where it would join the Leeds and Selby line at Sherburn-in-Elmet. 'The railway', he wrote, 'will one day intersect this country in almost every direction, I confidently believe, but there is so much terror.'

Most of all, Cayley has gone down in history as the true father of flight. In 1804 he built and successfully flew a model glider, later models featuring propellers powered by twisted rubber bands. Forty-four years later, a ten-year-old boy soared over Brompton Dale in a Cayley glider, the inventor regarding this as a test flight, and insisting he

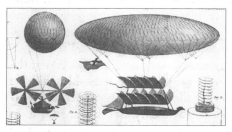

One of Sir George Cayley's Airship designs (from The Philosophical Magazine, 1817)

needed a fully-grown man to prove air navigation was feasible. At the age of seventy-nine, he cajoled his coachman into acting as pilot of his air machine. This was a full-sized glider fitted with inherent lateral and longitudinal stabilisers, an adjustable fin and tailplane, a car (like a manned balloon's) with an undercarriage, and pilot-operated controls, the basic features of every plane flying today. Local people crowded the Vale of Pickering to watch the great event. One asked, 'What's the good of it?' Cayley retorted: 'What's the good of a new-born baby?' The unhappy coachman was carried a distance of nearly 200 metres, and was so scared out of his wits that, on landing, he promptly handed in his notice, declaring he had been engaged to drive, not fly. In a prescient letter, Cayley, who made a careful study of aerodynamics, admitted that 'a hundred necks have to be broken before all the sources of accident can be ascertained and guarded against.'

The irony of Cayley's life was that the nation's most distinguished scientific body, the Royal Society, refused to accept him as a member. They later confessed that this was 'one of our most notable omissions'. They could say that again.

PERSECUTION

In 1571, at the age of fifteen, Margaret Middleton of York married John Clitherow, a butcher. Over the next few years she became a Catholic convert and was frequently imprisoned in York Castle for her religious activities. In her home she concealed priests on the run from the authorities, and she used a room in the house next door to her husband's shop in The Shambles for the holding of Mass, which was strictly illegal. The sheriff's men questioned local children and forced a boy staying with the family to reveal the location of the room, where they found incriminating altar beads, relics and vestments. Not wanting a child to be compelled to give evidence against her, Margaret refused to undergo trial by jury. Many neighbours pleaded for clemency, and even a judge wanted to release her, especially as she was rumoured to be pregnant. But her refusal to disclose the names of the priests she had harboured or of her helpers counted against her. On 25 March 1586, aged thirty, she was slowly and horrifically pressed to death by several hundredweights of stone placed on a door on top of her. In 1970 Margaret Clitherow was canonised, and she is now honoured by a small shrine and chapel at 35 The Shambles.

❉ ❉ ❉

GASMAN

A foretaste of the era of gaslight was provided as far back as 1684 by Dr John Clayton, rector of Crofton, near Wakefield, a scientist educated as a theologian, who realised that gases which developed in coal-pits and endangered miners' lives were combustible. He experimented with chunks of coal, which he roasted over a fire without allowing them to burn up, and found that the resulting gas gave off a pleasant, light flame. Clayton was the first person to place on record that the distillation of coal in a closed vessel produced an inflammable gas (which he called spirit of coal) that could not only be collected but stored in bladders. He seems to have been a prankish fellow. 'When I had in mind to divert strangers or friends,' he wrote, 'I have taken one of these bladders and pricking a hole thereon with a pin and compressing gently the bladder near the flame of a candle till it once took fire, it would continue flaming till all the spirit was compressed out of the bladder.' What larks.

CHAPTER 7

CRIME AND (SOMETIMES) PUNISHMENT

OLD BONES

Tall and refined, Eugene Aram was a schoolteacher of a poetic bent, a master of Latin, Greek and Hebrew who bestowed his knowledge on pupils at a school in Gouthwaite in the West Riding. After marrying a woman named Anna Spence, he moved to Knaresborough, where he started his own school. The couple had seven children, and, according to his students, he was a rigid disciplinarian and a stern upholder of the Christian faith. Out of school, however, his hobbies were petty thieving and receiving stolen goods. His accomplice was his next-door neighbour, William Houseman, a flax-dresser. On 7 February 1744, they brained with a pick one Daniel Clark (described as 'pockmarked, stammering and weedy'), who was foolishly carrying £200 of his wife's dowry. They squeezed the corpse, doubled up, under a rock in St Robert's Cave in Knaresborough, through which flowed the River Nidd. Since the two men had been seen in Clark's company on the night he vanished, Aram thought it sensible to quit the district, and, deserting his family, travelled first to Nottingham and then to London, where he caroused for twelve years, until a hankering to resume the academic life (or perhaps a shortage of cash) led him to seek a post at a grammar school in King's Lynn, Norfolk. Here, for £20 a year, he taught Latin.

In 1758 a labourer discovered what were believed to be Clark's bones. That same year a visitor from Knaresborough to King's Lynn recognised Aram, who promptly said the fellow was mistaken about his identity. Two months later, Houseman confessed that he and Aram had killed Clark and led local magistrates to the remains. Two constables informed by the visitor to King's

Lynn of Aram's whereabouts, brought him back in a chaise to Knaresborough, crowds meeting them as they rattled into town. Alighting from the chaise and seeing his wife and children for the first time in fourteen years, Aram strode up to them and said, 'Well, and how do you do?' Houseman had agreed to be a witness for the Crown, but Aram was kept in a York jail for almost a year until his trial. Preparing his defence in his cell, he made a particular study of a book *Monasticon Eboracense,* which dealt with relics of the saints. At the trail he claimed that the remains at St Robert's Well might well be the bones of a saint or hermit buried centuries earlier.

Found guilty of murder, he slashed his wrists with a razor the night before the execution. On a paper on his cell table he left a note justifying his suicide attempt: 'My life was not polluted, my morals were irreproachable, and my opinions were orthodox.' He was already half-dead when dragged to the hangman. His corpse was left dangling in a nearby forest, and his skull was presented to the College of Surgeons. Several years later, following doubts expressed in some quarters about his guilt, he was eulogised in a Thomas Hood poem, *The Dream of Eugene Aram,* which included the lines:

> 'Much study had made him very lean,
> And pale, and leaden-ey'd.'

❄ ❄ ❄

YOUR WIFE OR MINE?

Wife-swapping today is considered a practice favoured by a bored bourgeoisie. In South Yorkshire during the nineteenth century it was a common indulgence among humbler citizens, especially in mining communities. It had also been fashionable among the area's country folk at the beginning of the eighteenth century.

At that time Hatfield was an important community in the marshlands between Doncaster and Thorne, serving as a centre for the many small villages round and about. It boasted several ale-houses, one run by Elizabeth Dearman and her husband James. In the Archbishop of York's Consistory Court it was to be described as 'an odd house a distance from any town'.

In the court the couple were charged with keeping 'a disorderly and scandalous alehouse' where lewd persons, male and female, habitually resorted, and where Elizabeth had performed many wicked deeds. She was often, it seems, in the company of Allan Cockin, a married man, and it was clear that Messrs Dearman and Cockin had agreed to exchange wives for a consideration of seven shillings and sixpence. The ceremony involving Elizabeth and Cockin had taken place in the alehouse, where they retired to the same bed for the night.

In evidence, it emerged that the inn's reputation was so scandalous that magistrates had ordered its closure. Despite this, it continued to sell ale. A witness, Richard Woodcock, twenty-five years old and 'a gentleman', told of visiting the inn, where he found Cockin, Dearman and another man discussing the possibility of exchanging wives. Elizabeth approved the idea and the price was agreed, Cockin pulling the money from his pocket and handing it to Dearman. Cockin then asked someone in the bar to perform the ceremony. In return he would spend half-a-crown on drink for those present. Hearing this, an enthusiastic toper donned a long, white apron, representing a surplice, acquired a prayer-book and read out the contractual section of the marriage service. As soon as the ceremony was over, Elizabeth sat by Cockin's side, murmured, 'Now thou art my own' and pulled out coins to be spent on ale. In a conversation with her husband's nephew, Elizabeth said she 'loved Allan Cockin's little finger better than her husband James's body'.

Woodcock called Cockin a 'lewd and scandalous person who hath been indicted several times for sheep-stealing and other notorious crimes'. And Thomas Moore, a farmer, said that from 1709 to 1711 Dearman had kept a disorderly house where sheep-stealers were sheltered and entertained. Other guests were criminals who brought them stolen goods. At the 'marriage ceremony', he revealed, a customer had, at Elizabeth's request, acted as her father to give her away.

The local constable said that when he arrived to arrest Cockin, he had to kick the door down, and Elizabeth promptly hustled Cockin into the cellar.

Unhappily, no record of the outcome of this case has survived, though it has been suggested that a public penance was performed in the parish church.

Elizabeth died aged ninety.

MONEY FOR OLD ROPE

The attractive valley of Cragg Vale in Hebden Bridge was the realm of 'King David', otherwise David Hartley, leader of a notorious and proficient eighteenth-century gang of coin counterfeiters. At a time when gold was scarce, the Government had legalised foreign coins for circulation. One, the Portuguese 4,000-reis piece, was enthusiastically forged by Hartley and his men. It was made from chippings from guineas loaned to the coiners by dishonest friends at two shillings a time. A local Customs and Excise supervisor, William Dighton, obtained enough evidence from a paid informer to have Hartley arrested while he was drinking in the Old Cock in Halifax. His arrest was followed by Dighton's murder, possibly because some influential people feared they might be exposed as accessories and ruined. Joseph Harrison, the deputy chief constable of Halifax, was arrested but escaped. Two men charged with the murder were freed through lack of evidence, but were re-arrested and accused of highway robbery, as Dighton's pockets had been rifled. The men, Robert Thomas and Matthew Normanton, were convicted and hanged at York, their bodies afterwards suspended in chains on the 864-foot Beacon Hill dominating Halifax, their arms outstretched and fingers pointing to Bull Close Lane, where the killing had taken place. Hartley himself was executed and buried in Heptonstall churchyard, where his grave can still be seen.

FIDDLER ON THE TRAIN

Only a psychologist could hazard whether it was Charley Peace's gargoyle-like countenance (partially concealed in later life by a luxuriant beard) that led him into a life of crime. It must be admitted, however, that he was a person of some versatility. As well as being a skilled burglar, he played the violin, recited monologues, and was an ardent pacifist. In 1876, during a quarrel, he shot dead his next-door neighbour, with whose wife he had been associating, in the yard adjoining their homes in Banner Cross Terrace, Sheffield. From now on he was known as the Banner Cross Murderer. He fled south and found refuge in a house in Peckham, London, his legal wife occupying the basement, and 'Mr and Mrs Thompson' (Peace and one Susan Grey described as a 'dreadful woman for drink and snuff') upstairs. He disguised himself by walnut-staining his face, dyeing his hair black and donning spectacles. With his lady friend he regularly attended church and held musical soirées, at which the talented Peace would provide the entertainment. His repertoire of recitations probably included the elegy he wrote on his infant son's death:

> *Farewell, my dear son, by us all beloved*
> *Thou art gone to dwell in the mansions above.*
> *In the bosom of Jesus who sits on the throne*
> *Thou art anxiously waiting for us to come home . . .*

By night he would cram his burgling tools into his violin case, harness Tommy, his pony, to a trap, and, armed with a revolver, set out on housebreaking expeditions. After two years' success in this line of work, he was caught in a Blackheath garden by a constable he shot in the arm. His true identity having been established, he was bundled onto a train, to be tried at Leeds Assizes for the Sheffield murder. It proved an eventful journey.

The train was half a mile past Shireoak, a Midlands station, when two passengers, Mr William Barlow, a fruiterer, and a Mr Benjamin Cocker, heard a shout from the next compartment. Barlow tried to open his near-side window, but, this being an icy

THE NOTORIOUS BLACKHEATH BURGLAR

PEACE,

THE MURDERER OF Mr. ARTHUR DYSON, Civil Engineer, Banner Cross, Sheffield, November, 1876.

COPYRIGHT. TAKEN FROM LIFE.

Charley Peace

winter's day, found it frozen fast. He was luckier with the other window. Leaning out, he saw a man in prison officer's uniform staring out of the next window and holding a shoe. A second warder yelled that he had pulled the communication cord to no effect. Nothing happened when Cocker pulled his own cord. Then, at a siding, he and one of the warders waved to a signalman in his box, and the train ground to a halt.

Cocker realised that a prisoner, in fact Peace, had escaped from the train. Peace indeed had been restless throughout the journey and given endless trouble. Then, just as the express was speeding at 50 m.p.h. through Worksop, he had leapt to the window. One warder had grabbed his left foot and held on desperately, while the second had fruitlessly pulled the cord. For two miles the struggle had gone on, the prisoner hanging downwards with his ugly face bumping against the outside of the carriage as he tried to kick himself free of the warder's grip. At last he had managed to wriggle his left foot out of its shoe – still in the stupefied warder's grasp – and break free. In his clumsy fall his head struck the carriage footboard with terrible force, and he rolled over and down the bank in a cloud of dust. When the train stopped, the warders ran along the track to the spot where their prisoner had dropped. They found him lying semi-conscious on the line, his head badly injured. As, shortly afterwards, he was being hoisted into the guard's van of a Sheffield-bound goods train, he muttered, 'I'm cold. Cover me up.' The sympathetic warders obliged.

Convicted at the Assizes of the Sheffield murder, Peace confessed to another, years earlier, in Manchester. During his pre-execution breakfast he was calm, delivering a sanctimonious little homily to the warders on the Christian state of grace. The effect was somewhat diminished when he glowered at his plate and observed: 'This is bloody rotten bacon.'

❄ ❄ ❄

SANCTIONED SADISM

Among the exhibits at Whitby's Captain Cook Memorial Museum is a human hand dating back to the eighteenth century. Found over a lintel in a cottage at Castleton thirteen miles away, it is said to have been severed from the body of a hanged felon while he was still on the gibbet, and pickled in a preservative. It gets a mention in one of the Harry Potter books, *Chamber of Secrets*.

❄ ❄ ❄

TWO BAD GUYS

The very construction of Millgarth police station, the police head-quarters in Leeds, may be construed as a gesture of contempt towards the criminal fraternity. It occupies the site of what was once the home of Owney Madden, a local lad who crossed the Atlantic to become a feared gangster.

Madden was born in a cramped terraced house near the city's market. His father worked as a cloth-presser in a local sweat-shop and kept pigeons whose loft the young Owney regularly cleaned out. The family moved to Wigan, Liverpool and, eventually, New York. He was fourteen when he had his first experience of crime. A boy snipped the handles of his mother's shopping bag with a pair of scissors and scampered off with her groceries. Owney later told friends: 'When I saw what that kid had got away with, I decided I was a fool not to try myself.' He was soon running with violent street gangs and not unnaturally made enemies. At twenty-one he was gunned down by rivals in a dance-hall ambush. Though he fell with six bullets in his body, he discharged himself from hospital a week later, and within hours the three gang leaders who had ordered his elimination were dead.

Incongruously, Madden had a reputation for being mild-mannered and polite, his generosity inspiring loyalty among his acquaintances. The actor George Raft, well-known as an associate of gangsters, began his film career with money borrowed from Madden, and based his portrayals of coin-flipping hoods on the Yorkshireman. Madden also put up the cash that enabled Mae West to launch 'Sex', the first stage show she wrote herself. Ten years later she showed her gratitude by hiding him in her apartment when he was wanted by the law for questioning. Madden also ran the mobs who ruthlessly controlled the fighter Primo Carnera, and paid for young amateur boxers to sail to England to take part in friendly bouts. Most famously, Madden ran the Cotton Club, the spawning ground of the era's great jazz musicians.

Madden masterminded New York's bootleg barons, and became a dapper dresser who retained his Yorkshire ways and addressed his friends as 'Lad'. At the height of his nefarious activities he was keeping a pigeon-loft on the roof of the skyscraper that was his headquarters. Jailed on a manslaughter charge, he got out of Sing Sing after eight years, in time to see Raft give his Madden-based performance in *Each Dawn I Die*. Newspapers claimed he had greased Parole Board palms with an enormous bribe to obtain his release.

Madden finally surprised the forces of law and order by ostensibly retiring from crime and moving to Hot Springs, Arkansas, where he lived next door to a former police chief. He even joined the local chamber of commerce. For the next thirty years, however, he was shadowed by FBI agents, who were convinced he was running a vast, illegal racing wire service. On the other hand, he was credited with keeping the Mafia out of the town. He died aged seventy-four, still carrying in him the bullets from the dance-hall shooting. Shortly before his death, Mae West admitted he had been her 'hottest affair'.

Another Yorkshireman who led a disreputable life across the Atlantic was Ben Thompson, born in 1843 in Knottingley, where life was tough and jobs difficult to find. His father was a sailor, and despite the family's poverty Ben and his younger brother Billy had a good education, Ben taking his studies seriously. Though he and Billy were skilled street-fighters, Ben was literate (an unusual working-class accomplishment for the time) and good at maths. Just before his sixteenth birthday, the family learned of the murder of a relative in Texas. In his will he left Ben's father a large sum on condition that he came over to care for his four orphans. In 1860, at the age of eighteen, Ben, the immigrant, was among a group that chased Indians who had kidnapped five children. He shot down the Indian leader and the children were rescued unharmed. On another occasion he stole a shotgun and shot in the back a black boy who had made fun of Billy. Because of the racial bias of Texas courts at that time, he was sentenced to a derisory six months' jail and a $100 fine. On his release, his father thrashed him, telling him that a Yorkshireman always looked his victim in the eye. Ben pledged that from now on he would always draw his gun first but shoot second. He became a prolific gunslinger, killing sixteen men in all, more often than not as a law enforcer, though his lethal temper made him feared equally by the good and the bad. The famous lawman Bat Masterton described him as a deadly operator, with nerves of steel. Accused of cheating in a card game with some Mexican soldiers, he responded, 'Get knotted', before shooting two soldiers, one after the other. When he shot down a club owner, Thompson stood over him and, in a broad Yorkshire accent, said, 'Eee, lad, tha'll not be pullin' a shotgun on me again.' The shooting led to his arrest for murder, but, after a long trial, he was acquitted. Thompson's own life ended when he was ambushed in a booth of a San Antonio theatre and gunned down by three assassins.

A WEDDING TO REMEMBER

On 24 November 1617, a wedding took place in the village chapel at Cawthorne, near Barnsley. Following an ancient custom, a number of boys barred the exit of the bride and her party, who would not be allowed to emerge until they had paid a ransom of a shilling, or at least sixpence. (The groom had already left.) Being poor, the bride offered threepence, but eventually was constrained to hand over fourpence. Declaring that this was insufficient, the boys locked the party in the chapel, leaving the bride and her friends and relations to wonder how they could possibly ride to the Barnsley reception before dark. The only possible way out was through the bell-house door: but not for long, as the boys set to work and propped a beam against it. To aggravate matters, the boys said that if they did not receive sixpence they would pull off the bride's left shoe (though, as she was locked in, it is not clear how they expected to manage this). At long last the groom and several friends succeeded in breaking open the great south door and hustled the bride and her party out. Meanwhile, the bride's sympathetic employer, James Bottomley, removed two boys who had squeezed through the melée into the chapel. One small boy called the party Puritans and compounded the insult by bidding the Devil go with them. The influential grandfather of one of the lads later accused Bottomley of assault. The case, in the Consistory Court at York, dragged on for an incredible two years. Charges and countercharges of collusion, corruption, defamation and prevarication were levelled. There were also accusations of manipulation of witnesses and clerical misbehaviour. The chapel curate was persuaded to give evidence for one boy, whose father knew that the reverend gentleman had in the past performed clandestine marriages and other illegal acts like altering birth dates in the parish register. A notary public appointed to represent the boys said most of Bottomley's witnesses were paupers 'and not worth even ten shillings in debtless goods'. Sadly, the outcome of this interminable case is not known, as the court papers that have survived the centuries are incomplete. Scholars, however, believe that, in view of what must have been horrendous costs on both sides, a compromise was reached.

❊   ❊   ❊

HEADS DOWN

All over the country felons were hanged. Only in Halifax were they beheaded. A machine resembling the French guillotine (which it anticipated by 600 years) stood on a platform near the town's western exit, reached by a flight of stone steps. The platform was buried when the instrument went out of use, but in 1839 workmen clearing the area found two skeletons with severed heads.

The machine consisted of two 15-foot posts joined at the top by a beam holding them four feet apart. At ground level stood an execution block on which the unfortunate criminal was obliged to lay his head between the posts. The movable block had an eighteen-inch-long axe blade attached to its lower edge, and was drawn to the top of the posts by a peg. The criminal was tied to a rope attached to the peg, and, when he was pushed forward, the peg was jerked out, the blade dropped, and the victim thus became, in a sense, his own executioner. If no one could be found willing to do the pushing, a team of volunteers was recruited to pull the rope simultaneously, so that any repugnance at the taking of a life would be shared (as with the firing squads of later years). At a time when stealing was a capital offence, the instrument was intended to discourage thieves who might feel tempted to steal wool and cloth hung out to dry on frames outside cottages after being scoured or washed. The persistent use of the machine led to the thieves' litany, 'From Hell, Hull and Halifax, good Lord deliver us', referring to the horrors of Hell, the prison at Hull and the dread machine at Halifax.

The only way a victim could escape the guillotine was to withdraw his head before the blade fell and then escape over a brook across the parish boundary. He could then remain free provided he did not return. One criminal escaped this way, but foolishly returned seven years later and was duly executed in 1623. He is commemorated by a pub, The Running Man. A 15-foot replica of the guillotine now stands on the original Gibbet Street site, and the original blade, reverently renovated, is now preserved as part of another replica in the Pre-Industrial Museum in the Piece Hall.

❅ ❅ ❅

THE MAN WHO FIRED THE MINSTER

Early on the frosty morning of 2 February 1829, a young chorister arrived at York Minster for his usual practice. Finding the great doors still closed, he passed the time sliding on the ice in the yard. Slipping, he fell on his back. Lying there, he saw smoke billowing from the Minster roof, clearly from a fire raging within. Scrambling to his feet, he raced off to find the sexton.

The news that the Minster was burning spread through the city and in minutes an enormous crowd had gathered. They watched the arrival of the Minster's own horse-drawn fire- engine and the firefighters' subsequent attempt to quell the blaze. The damage, it soon became clear, was horrific. Parts of the central aisle, all interior work from the organ to the altar screen, the stalls, the gallery, the bishop's throne and the pulpit had been almost completely destroyed. The firemen summoned help from Leeds and other towns, while a strong force of soldiers and citizens tried to help extinguish the flames. The bells of St Michael-le-Belfry sounded the tocsin and the crash of falling timbers and masonry contributed to the mayhem. It took several hours before the fire was finally under control. Damage was estimated at £70,000, including the loss of centuries-old, beautifully crafted artefacts.

Inside the Minster a knotted rope was found, which, together with pincers and matches, suggested an arsonist had been at work. Suspicion soon fell on Jonathan Martin, a well-known religious fanatic who had often denounced the 'deceivers of the House of God'. For some time he had haunted the Minster, often leaving behind badly spelled notes addressed to 'you dark and lost clergymen' whose 'blind, hellish doctrine' he condemned. A widespread search failed to find Martin in York. The hunt was extended and a £100 reward offered for his apprehension. A few days later he was picked up sixty miles away at Cadlow Hill, near Hexham in Northumberland, whither he had trudged from York. He at once admitted he had started the fire, was arrested and was brought back to the scene of his crime. When examined by magistrates, he was completely composed, justifying himself as God's appointed agent. He spoke of two

York Minster arsonist Jonathan Martin in jail, with his autograph. W. Walton after Rev. T. Kilby: (Courtesy of York City Art Gallery)

dreams he had had. In one a man shot an arrow into the Minster door. In the other a cloud dropped onto the Minster and then over his house, which trembled. When he awoke, he decided the 'Hand of God' had ordered him to set fire to the great cathedral. To ensure no innocent party was blamed, he had stolen throne hangings and curtains found in his possession.

Why the long walk to Hexham? This was the town in which he was born. Other details of his early life emerged. As a young man he had travelled to London where he was press-ganged and forced to serve aboard ships on which he would have endured all the hardships commonly experienced by seamen at that time. As a result of all this, he said, he began to have 'visions and revelations', though it was thought that a bad fall and serious head injury he had suffered at sea might have damaged his brain. At his Assizes trial he was found not guilty on the grounds of insanity and sent to an asylum, where he died nine years later.

Martin had a brother John, a notable artist who specialised in apocalyptic paintings with such titles as 'The Great Day Of His Wrath', 'The Fall of Babylon' and 'The Last Judgement'. Jonathan too enjoyed sketching and painting. At his trial some of his drawings were produced, and, while he was in jail, he was visited by sightseers who carried off his autographed pictures as souvenirs.

❊   ❊   ❊

NOW WILL YOU BEHAVE?

A form of punishment meted out in the Yorkshire Dales and Wolds towards the end of the nineteenth century was known as Riding the Stang. The basic idea was to ridicule a domestic offender, particularly a man in the habit of beating his wife or being unfaithful to her. An effigy was made of the offender and around its neck was hung a placard providing details of his misconduct. The effigy was placed on a long wooden pole or ladder. Villagers slammed pots and pans as loudly as possible, while one of their number climbed the ladder or pole to sing or recite a verse narrating the offence. The whole caboodle was then carried through the village and three times around the parish church, one important step along the way being the offender's house. Ridings of the Stang took place on three successive, noisy nights, following which the effigy was burned. And that was the end of the matter. Miscreants subjected to this treatment were said to have been 'well and truly stanged'.

❊   ❊   ❊

THE BOOTLEGGERS

Saltburn in the late eighteenth century was an isolated hamlet not far from the shore, enclosed by towering cliffs and inhabited by fisherfolk. Aside from netting cod, the tiny community also earned a decent living as smugglers. At the centre of their illicit trade was John Andrew, landlord of the Ship Inn, and popularly known as King of the Smugglers, a title rumoured to have been bestowed on him by his admiring daughter. Oddly, there is not a single reference to Andrew in the Customs records of the period, which may well be a tribute to his success, until his final capture.

Andrew came from a Scottish farming family and was brought up in the Montrose area, itself a notorious smugglers' haunt, which suggests he had early lessons in the skills required by his chosen profession. He seems to have arrived in Saltburn in 1780, quietly settling in as mine host at the Ship, which, with its splendid position on the sands, must have made an excellent centre for smuggling operations, and an obvious rendezvous for the bootleggers themselves.

John Andrew reputedly linked up with one Thomas King, a brewer who was believed to be the local smugglers' leader. Andrew's daughter cemented the relationship by marrying King. After some early successes, the two men are said to have invested in a lugger, the *Morgan Butler*, whose master, a Captain Brown, had a reputation as a brave sailor who was, however, not averse to exercising violence in the pursuit of his illicit activities.

In 1804 Andrew was commissioned as an ensign in the Third Regiment of the Cleveland Volunteer Infantry, and, in less than five years, was a captain in the local militia, who, ironically, were occasionally called out to support the hard-pressed Customs men. Andrew's profits from his smuggling operations enabled him to buy the White House, an imposing farmhouse overlooking Saltburn, in whose cellars he stored smuggled goods. A false floor in a stable stall gave access to the cellars in which the euphemistically named Free Traders stored their barrels of duty-free rum and gin from Holland. When Customs men arrived to search the premises, Andrew's gang tugged into the stall a mare they could trust to launch a vicious kick at any intruder.

By 1817 the Cleveland Hunt had appointed Andrew its Master of Foxhounds. So accepted was he by the local gentry that he was said to have supplied a large part of the wedding trousseau of a local peer's daughter. At this time there was a trade embargo on all French goods, and the obliging Andrew was able to provide his fellow Hunt members with many luxuries from across the Channel, such as brandy, wine, silks, lace and gloves.

But Andrew's luck was running out. In the early summer of 1827 he was caught landing a consignment near Hornsea. On conviction, he was fined, though how much is not known, reports varying from £1,000 to £100,000. Whatever the sum, he was unable to drum up the cash, and he ended up in York Castle, where he remained imprisoned for two years, until influential friends, of which there was no scarcity, negotiated his release.

Robin Hood's Bay in the days of its smuggling notoriety

One eighteenth-century historian commented, 'Show me a fisherman and I'll show you a smuggler.' This was true along the Yorkshire coast, including such attractive harbours as Robin Hood's Bay, which boasted a community immersed in 'free trade'. When landed, the goods they smuggled quickly disappeared into cellars and specially constructed hidey-holes in the cottages that lined the narrow lanes and alleys. More than any other coastal village, Robin Hood's Bay had a long, and, in the circumstances, understandable reputation for hostility to outsiders. At least one Revenue coble was continuously anchored there, though at one stage the Customs Surveyor had been forced to buy one himself as the Customs Board had refused to fund such a vessel. Their footling excuse was that the port was too small to bother about. In fact, Robin Hood's Bay proved the bane of Customs men for at least a century, the smugglers stooping to a variety of tricks in their attempts to fool investigators. When one vessel in the Bay was searched, officers found gallons of brandy in the hold, buried beneath heaps of salt. In 1772 a Whitby port officer found, in one Robin Hood's Bay cottage, smuggled tea on a bed, under the garret stairs and in an open cupboard. The smugglers in this case seem to have been singularly careless. Most local cottages boasted secret cupboards that suited their purpose admirably.

By the autumn of 1773, a schooner, a cutter and two dinghies were busy landing smuggled goods in the Bay. A year later the *Yorkshire Gazette* was complaining:

> The practice of smuggling increases amazingly in these parts. It has become so general that seizures are almost daily made, and many people of supposed good circumstances are known to deal largely in the pernicious trade. If the contraband trade is suffered to go on it will inevitably drain the County of a great part of its money and endanger the lives and morals of its inhabitants.

It may have been this editorial that persuaded the War Office to send troops into the area to support the Revenue men. Initially, this seemed to have little effect. In 1779 Excise officers seized 260 casks of brandy, gallons of geneva (a Dutch spirit), fifteen bags of tea and a chest full of blunderbusses, pistols and cutlasses. The enraged smugglers fought back, but eventually scuttled off, leaving their firearms behind, when soldiers marched in. By the early nineteenth century there were more than thirty revenue cutters operating around the coast, and the smugglers' days were soon numbered.

They are now remembered at a heritage centre, The Saltburn Smugglers, near the Ship Inn, where John Andrew once presided.

AN UNDESERVING HERO

The York-based *Yorkshire Evening Press* has published a series of columns under the by-line Dick Turpin. Why anyone should adopt the name of this squalid character as a pseudonym is hard to imagine. Turpin was far from the romantic hero of tradition.

An alehouse keeper's son, Turpin was apprenticed to a butcher, but, having been caught cattle-stealing, he joined a notorious Essex gang of deer thieves and smugglers. When the gang broke up, Turpin went into partnership with Tom King, a well-known highwayman, whom he accidentally killed while firing, by some accounts, at a constable, and, by others, at an innkeeper. Turpin escaped to Yorkshire, where, under his mother's name of Palmer, he procured and sold horses. Early in 1739 he was committed to York Castle on suspicion of horse-stealing. Tried at the city Assizes for the theft of a black mare and foal, he was convicted and sentenced to death. Apart from King's killing, for which he expressed regret, he also admitted one murder and several robberies. Most of his associates having predeceased him, he uttered the wise homily: 'There is no union so liable to dissolution as that of felons.' After paying five men three pounds ten shillings to follow the cart bearing his body, he was duly executed. He was buried in St George's churchyard, York, and his 28-pound fetters are still on view in the York Castle Museum.

In his romance *Rookwood*, the writer Harrison Ainsworth gave a spirited account of Turpin's ride from London to York on his mare, Black Bess. This now legendary incident is pure fiction.

CHAPTER 8

ROYAL AFFAIRS

THE PRINCESS AND THE PLUMBER

In 1894, the twenty-two-year-old Princess Alix of Hesse-Darmstadt, later to become Alexandra, the last Tsarina of Russia, paid a spring visit to Harrogate to take the waters. She booked into a boarding-house managed by Christopher Allen, who also ran a plumbing business. Reserving her rooms through a local estate agent, she at first assumed the name of Baroness Startenburg, but word of her true identity spread, and on her first evening she was accosted by an autograph-hunter. Her visit was reported in detail not by the London dailies but, the following year, by an obscure publication, *Armstrong's Harrogate Almanack*. This records that, on her second day, the princess discovered that Allen's wife, Emma, was confined to her bed. Alix's secretary, Baroness Fabrice, anxiously asked Allen if the malady was 'anything infectious'. He duly replied that he could not say. His wife had, in fact, just given birth to twins. 'As twins – even the best of twins – are not the most charming neighbours at any time,' the *Almanack* observed, 'and least of all when one goes to a watering place for quiet and rest, it would not have been surprising if the visitors had at once decided to pack up and seek fresh quarters.' The princess, however, took the news 'in the most agreeable manner', announcing that it was a good luck omen (an early hint, perhaps, of the streak of mysticism later to lead to her ruinous dependence, as Tsarina, on the mad monk Rasputin). Instead of making a hasty departure to one of Harrogate's palatial hotels, she stayed at the rooming-house for a month. While there, the Allens later told an *Almanack* interviewer, she 'tripped and sang . . . like a happy English girl just home from school'. Occasionally, she would pop into her room to help an alarmed servant make the bed. She would also startle Emma Allen by tapping on the kitchen door to ask if she might come in. Dandling the twins affectionately or standing with her back to the fire, she would chat about Mrs Allen's cooking and express her fondness for Yorkshire puddings. She travelled to the sulphur baths in an open chaise, but left in a cab, to avoid catching a chill. At the baths, she revelled in listening to other clients gossiping about her in adjoining cubicles. She would also take long rides in one of the three-wheeled, self-propelled bathchairs then popular in fashionable spas. For entertainment she watched performance dogs and Punch and Judy and minstrel shows.

So involved did the princess become with the newborn twins that for one of them she knitted and embroidered a christening gown. She also insisted on standing in as their godmother at the local church baptism, with the mayor and a butcher acting as godfathers. At her request the babies were named Nicholas (the name of her fiancé, the future Tsar) and Alix. Her christening presents included gold sleeve-links for the boy, and a gold, heart-shaped

Items presented to the Harrogate Pump Room Museum

(Courtesy of *Daily Telegraph*)

anklet, with a central pearl, for the girl. To the parents she presented photographs of herself and Nicholas, asking that they be kept until the children grew up, so that they might remember after whom they were named. Another photograph went to her baths attendant. Later that year she married and became Tsarina. But she never forgot the children, to whom she sent regular gifts. Immediately after her coronation she despatched beautifully enamelled cutlery, a napkin ring and a spoon. On their first birthday the twins received matching goblets. Gifts arrived for their confirmation at the age of ten, and for their twenty-first birthday in 1915, a gold cross and chain, inscribed 'Save and Keep' in Slavonic script and 'With God's Blessing, Alexandra of Russia, 31 May 1915,' arrived from Petrograd (now St Petersburg). Nicholas Allen became a bank manager, and his sister and her husband owned two Glasgow cinemas. The twins were not particularly friendly in later life, and both died in the 1970s. Many of the gifts from the tragic Tsarina (assassinated in 1917 by the Bolsheviks) are on view in Harrogate's Royal Pump Room Museum. They were presented by Nicholas's son Michael Allen, a retired advertising executive. Being a bank manager, he said, his father had kept the gifts in his own strong-room. Michael felt they should be returned to the town where the story began.

❄ ❄ ❄

CHEER!

When Queen Victoria accepted an invitation to open the new Leeds town hall in 1858, the city was ecstatic. It was decided to re-colour the mayor's twenty-year-old chain. Two carriages were prepared for council officials, one providing room for the town clerk's servant. There were so many applications for tickets of admission to the event that several were refused. Among the unlucky applicants were Leeds Infirmary's medical officer, the Yorkshire Inspector of Schools and the secretary of Leeds Stock

Exchange. Some requests were remarkably persuasive. The secretary of a local mechanics' institute called attention to the 'well-known liberality' of its chairman 'towards the cause of education amongst the working classes'. The plea fell on deaf ears. Another applicant, aged seventy-seven, wrote that he regularly attended the Sunday School of an Ebenezer Chapel: 'I was there last Sabbath and will attend as long as I am able, as I fully believe there would have been a revolution in this country but for Sabbath School and the benefits both Children and Parents have from them.' He is believed to have got his ticket.

The opening, it was agreed, would be combined with an exhibition in the Cloth Hall of the work of local factories, and a music festival beginning with Mendelssohn's *Elijah* and ending with Handel's *Messiah*. There would also be a grand ball. Leeds itself was festooned with floral decorations and streamers and the royal route marked with triumphal arches, one a copy of London's Marble Arch.

On the eve of the big day the Queen, Prince Albert and the Princesses Alice and Helena arrived in a station whose seats were covered with scarlet cloth. Among those assembled to greet her was the mayor, Peter Fairbairn, who, according to one eye-witness, was adorned 'in such pomp and regal splendour as to resemble and recall to memory those visions of the past of which we read in story', such as the de Medicis. The observer went on: 'This grandeur would have ruined any man of ordinary appearance, but the Mayor, with his fine, upright carriage, snowy hair, and long flowing white beard, became it admirably.'

The day was drizzly with cold gusts of wind. Nonetheless, thousands gathered to cheer and throw their hats and handkerchieves into the air 'as if they were demented'. There was 'a very Babel of merriment'. The only snag was that none of the *hoi polloi* were allowed to approach Woodsley House, the mayor's residence, behind which a guard of honour was encamped.

For the big ceremony the next day, the police, who lined up as a barrier in front of the crowd, wore sprigs of holly and laurel, and white gloves. Children stood on two huge platforms on either side of the royal cortège. Men carried large boards on which were

Leeds during Queen Victoria's visit

printed various injunctions for the little ones: 'Prepare to cheer!', 'Sing!', 'Silence!' and 'Dismiss!'

At the town hall itself the crowds were so huge that barricades buckled, cracked and splintered under the pressure. The spectacle left a correspondent of *The Times* at a loss for the words which were his stock-in-trade. To essay a description, he wrote, would 'merely exhaust superlatives without result, for the "tremendous cheers" in print, and tremendous cheers in Leeds are widely different things'. The excitement was so intense as to be, according to one report, painful. Even the thunderous playing of the national anthem on the town hall organ was drowned by the applause for Her Majesty. She reciprocated by knighting the mayor on the spot.

The town hall today, apart from being a municipal centre, is the venue for assorted musical events. Critics complain of its 'bathroom acoustics'.

STRIKE!

On a morning in 1893, the children of Mornington Road primary school in Bingley stood outside the building chanting that they refused to come in for their lessons. They were, in fact, on strike. They were supported by their parents, who paraded on the other side of the road, barracking the teachers. At length, the head reluctantly capitulated and the children trotted merrily off. This case of industrial action was prompted by a royal event, the wedding of the Duke of York on that day. The children were insisting on a holiday to celebrate the occasion. The incident was duly and perhaps teeth-grittingly recorded in one of the school's now ancient log-books.

❄ ❄ ❄

BERTIE'S BACCARAT BLUNDER

In September 1890, a Hull shipowner, Arthur Wilson, decided to throw an exclusive house party at his local palatial residence, Tranby Croft, a name that, unfortunately for Wilson, was to become notorious. His guests were a number of aristocrats and, most prestigious of all, the Prince of Wales, later to become Edward VII but now chummily known to his circle as Bertie. The house was convenient for the racing at Doncaster, including the St Leger, which all the guests attended with some enthusiasm. Back at Tranby Croft, they all agreed to take part in a game of baccarat, which was then highly fashionable but illegal. Bertie agreed to act as banker, dealing from a box known as a 'shoe'. His chips had the Prince of Wales feathers embossed in gilt.

One of the players was Colonel Sir William Gordon-Cumming, a forty-one-year-old baronet, landowner, soldier and philanderer, renowned for his considerable charm. Another player was Wilson's son, Arthur, who was one of the colonel's subalterns. Young Arthur's consternation may be imagined when he clearly saw his superior officer cheating. Arthur turned to another officer and said: 'By God! This is too hot. The man next to me is cheating.' Wilson then told his mother, his sister and his brother-in-law.

The five people in the know decided to set a test. The following evening they played baccarat again, keeping a concerted eye on the colonel. Each became sure they saw him cheat. They told the other guests, who confronted Gordon-Cumming. He heatedly denied the charge and begged to see Bertie. The two men then had a brief conversation. 'I have heard certain persons have brought a foul and abominable charge against me,' exclaimed the colonel. 'I have to emphatically deny that I have done anything of the kind.' No sympathy was forthcoming from the Prince. Instead Gordon-Cumming was required to sign a pledge that he would never play cards for money again. He vociferously protested, but was told this was the only way to avoid a scandal in which the Prince would be embroiled. Though this was patently untrue, Gordon-Cumming signed, and the document was sent to the Prince's private secretary for safe keeping.

Within a few weeks, however, fashionable society was buzzing with the story. Only one course of action was open to Gordon-Cumming: to sue his five accusers for slander.

Opening on 1 June 1891, the case lasted a week, much to the joy of a salivating Press. It was held before the Lord Chief Justice, Lord Coleridge, who distributed tickets among his friends, as if it were a pantomime. The proceedings may have been damaging to Gordon-Cumming but they were even worse for Bertie, who was forced to admit he had spent much of his time in Hull playing an illegal card-game. Gordon-Cumming also had to endure the obvious prejudice of the judge. Though Bertie was a witness against the colonel, Lord Coleridge placed him in a red leather armchair by his side, and entertained him to lunch every day of the trial.

The jury took thirteen minutes to find that Gordon-Cumming had no case. He was ordered to pay costs, resigned his commission and was socially ruined. Bertie had to put up with a newspaper cartoon that changed the Prince of Wales' motto from 'I Serve' to 'I Deal'.

Tranby Croft is now the home of Hull High School, where it may be safely assumed baccarat is not on the sporting curriculum. Another Yorkshire link with the Prince of Wales is to be found at Saltburn, where he and Lillie Langtry, the actress who became his mistress, are said to have had secret trysts. Their rendezvous was reportedly a large sandstone villa on a cliff, with fine views of the coast and the sea. Originally called The Cottage, it is now known as Teddy's Nook. It received this disrespectful name in the 1920s, a decade or so after King Edward VII's death.

CHAPTER 9

BIG BUSINESS

THE YORKSHIRE BALLOON

On a street in Calais a messenger from England approached a shabby elderly man in self-imposed exile and handed him a letter. Tears rolled down the old man's cheeks as he opened the envelope to find that it contained a banknote. 'God bless you,' he said. 'This will ease me.' He took his new acquaintance to his small bed-sitter, whose landlady clearly held her boarder in contempt, sat him down in the sparsely-furnished room and left him there while he went out to buy tea, bread and a cooked chicken. On his return he laid the table and treated the messenger to a modest meal. The old man reminisced. In his youth, he said, he had worked in a little draper's shop in York. If only, he mourned, he had never left it. 'Never aim, my dear sir, too high,' he sighed. When he accompanied his guest to the railway station, he happened to see there an English duke who recognised him, greeted him and handed him another banknote, for which he was duly grateful.

The old man was George Hudson, the financier who became the driving force behind the creation of Britain's burgeoning network of railways, and had been known, with good reason, as the Railway King. Now he was in penury and disgrace, a victim of his contempt for the code of basic business ethics.

In his early teens, Hudson, a Yorkshire farmer's son, had left his village home to work as an apprentice at the York draper's. By the age of twenty he was a partner in the business. He was twenty-seven when a great-uncle made him an enormous bequest, transforming Hudson into one of York's wealthiest citizens. Though ill-educated (throughout his life he persisted in dropping his aitches), he became interested in local politics, and, in 1833, now in his early thirties, became a director of a York bank that boasted capital of half a million pounds. That same year he attended a meeting that was to change his own and his country's destiny. Those present set up a company that would campaign for a railway line into York. Hudson was elected treasurer.

From the start, money was the mainspring of his existence. He had an enormous respect for the power it brought. A natural Conservative, he blotted his copybook during a general election by mailing gold sovereigns to poor people who had been induced to vote for the Tory candidate. Now known as the Tory 'briber-in-chief', he was summoned before a House of Commons select committee, which decided to forget his conduct for the simple reason that his political opponents, the Whigs, had also resorted to dubious tactics.

Hudson's railway ambitions received a boost when he became chairman of the new York and Midland Company, whose mission was to bring train services into York. After a spell as a council alderman he was also elected the city's first Tory Lord Mayor, irking opponents who resented this upstart's insults. When some complained that he deliberately excluded them from civic functions, he retorted that they were toadies touting for meals and invitations who had a bad habit of backbiting and, out of malice, invented conversations that had never taken place.

Though his election to a second term as Lord Mayor was found to be illegal, this proved merely academic, and Hudson vigorously pursued both civic and railway interests, wisely seeing the possibility of regular train services transforming Whitby and Scarborough into popular resorts. His tactics were frequently unpleasant. When he was denied control of the Hull and Selby line, he financed the revival of a defunct steamboat company to provide the line with stiff competition. Following the deaths of two passengers in a collision on a Hudson-owned line, the cause was said to be an elderly, short-sighted engine-driver, and the Press charged Hudson with sacrificing safety to cheeseparing economies. He was forgiven when large shareholders' dividends were announced. When it was proposed that professional auditors be appointed, he said he had never heard of such a thing. The directors, he pointed out, always audited the accounts and the books were open for inspection. Yet he drew support from the unlikeliest sources, among them the Brontë sisters, who bought shares. They might have been less enthusiastic had they known that Hudson not only employed unskilled engine-drivers, but allowed boys to man junction points, sacking anyone who protested. When accidents occurred, Hudson blamed conspiracies among workers. Delays and breakdowns he attributed to sabotage, such as the pouring of oatmeal into engines.

By the age of forty-four, Hudson had business interests not only in railways, but in farms, shops, banks, quarries, coal-mines and glassworks. His appearance and manners illustrated his overweening status. He was burly and rotund, with short legs and, said one observer, a 'sinister leer' in his eyes. He was also humourless, uncouth, domineering, ruthless, rude and tactless, regarding displays of sensitivity as signs of weakness. To complex questions he would reply with monosyllables. He dressed ostentatiously (favouring white waistcoats), and, when he walked, swung his arms like a sergeant-major. His energy was unquenchable. He tucked into huge meals and drank too much.

By the time the Midland Railway was formed, with Hudson as chairman, he was a national figure, controlling the country's largest rail system. He was dubbed the Railway Napoleon: certainly, in view of his dictatorial style, more accurate than King. In the course of his career he attracted a variety of sobriquets. To Thomas Carlyle he was a 'big swollen gambler'. He had homes in both Yorkshire and London, and, though the aristocracy flocked to his Knightsbridge residence, Londoners dismissed him as the Yorkshire Balloon. Similarly contemptuous was the renowned wit, Sydney Smith, who, in a letter to a friend, referred to Hudson as 'the retired Linen Draper'. Deriding his political acumen, a weekly paper, *The Yorkshireman*, described him as 'a sort of political Lilliputian in the land of Gulliver's adventures'. Mocking his white waistcoats, the Irish leader Daniel O'Connell, likened him to 'a turbot . . . sitting on its tail with its belly outwards'. At Oxford University, Hudson's eldest son became the Prince of Rails.

But to many of the citizens of York he remained a hero. When he masterminded the building of a new street to improve the station approach, it was named Hudson Street. A correspondent to the *Railway Times*, however, warned: 'Shareholders should be cautious ere they raise a railway autocrat, with power greater than the Prime Minister.' The same journal had already given Hudson a leading rôle in an imaginary opera, *Midas*, the opening chorus being sung at a grand railway amalgamation meeting. When, in 1845, the York to Scarborough line was officially opened exactly as Hudson had predicted, the inaugural train was hauled by two locos named Hudson and Lion and made its way via a tiny station he had built at Howsham, perhaps (unusually for him) for sentimental reasons, since this was the obscure village in which he had been born.

Provincial politics eventually proved inadequate for Hudson's ego, and he offered himself as Tory Parliamentary candidate for Sunderland. The *Manchester Guardian* said he knew as much about political economy as if he had just 'dropped from the moon'. In a speech to electors, he said that the fact that he had made a fortune made him deserving of their votes. He was duly elected, and when copies of *The Times* carrying the election news arrived in Sunderland by train, he threw copies of the paper at the assembled crowd, crying: 'See the march of intellect!' and 'See the power of steam!'

When Hudson and his family arrived back in York, they were greeted by a salute of cannon-fire. More honour came his way with his appointment as Deputy Lord Lieutenant of Durham. At a subsequent meeting in his constituency, which he pledged to provide with a new dock and railway, the chairman said: 'Mr Hudson is just the sort of man who *ought* to be rich. He is a sort of Chancellor of the Exchequer in railway matters.' When Charles Dickens became editor of a new paper, the *Daily News*, Hudson supplied it with information about the railways, even though its politics were opposed to his own.

One company in which Hudson was not involved was the Eastern Counties Railway, with lines from London to Colchester and Cambridge, which had a reputation for frequent accidents. *Punch* suggested that every criminal awaiting execution should have his sentence commuted to an Eastern Counties journey. A deputation called on Hudson, who kindly consented to become chairman. By 1846, most of the lines north of Leeds and east of the Pennines belonged to Hudson. Now that the nation's most beautiful scenery had been made available to the masses, said Hudson at his most grandiloquent, they 'could not but lift the mind from nature to nature's God'. On the ceremonial opening of Hudson's branch line to Bridlington, an East Riding admirer adapted Pope's epigram on Sir Isaac Newton:

When railways and railway shares were dark as night,
Men said that Hudson ruled and all was right.

But the seeds of Hudson's eventual destruction were being sown as, little by little, details emerged of his cavalier attitude to money and his dubious business methods. One of his railways, it was charged, did not abide by safety regulations. When accused of running trains late, he would produce figures which showed that, if the number of minutes by which trains had run *early* were subtracted from the minutes by which they had run *late*, the average lateness of his trains was insignificant. Charles Dickens, whose newspaper had profited from Hudson's news tips, now turned against him. To a friend the author wrote: 'I find a burning disgust arising in my mind – a sort of morbid canker of the most frightful description – against Mister Hudson. His position seems to me to be such a monstrous one, and so illustrative of the breeches pocket side of the English character, that I can't bear it.'

But the message, it seemed was not getting through to the *electors*, as, at a general election, Hudson retained his Parliamentary seat. By now his greed was on a monumental scale, and the corrupt Railway King was becoming immersed in a morass of complex business frauds. To make matters worse, by 1848 the great railway mania had fizzled out, with thousands of small investors ruined. There were now more than 5,000 miles of track in Britain, nearly 1,500 of which were under Hudson's control. His money and George Stephenson's engineering genius had not only changed the nation's landscape, but had transformed its industrial and social history. But now, even among his admirers, Hudson's prestige was on the wane. As dividends slumped, doubts about his management skills and honesty surfaced. For investors as greedy as himself he became a handy scapegoat. He was accused of flouting company laws and making undue profits on shares. One of his aides, it was discovered, had asked a traffic manager to exaggerate profits 'in order to make things pleasant'. As Brian Bailey wrote in

"Off the Rail": An 1849 Punch cartoon depicting Railway King George Hudson's fall from Grace.

his 1995 biography *George Hudson: The Rise and Fall of the Railway King*, these revelations spelled Hudson's doom. *The Yorkshireman* jumped on the bandwagon with the comment: 'His whole life has been one vast aggregation of avaricious . . . jobbing for the accumulation of wealth.' A report on one of Hudson's railway companies showed he had paid dividends to shareholders out of their own capital 'for the purpose of bolstering up the reputation of . . . this foul Charlatan'. He was even found to have cheated on his expenses. New charges dribbled out with awesome regularity. He had appropriated shares to which he was not entitled, and, due to irregularities in the accounts, the York and North Midland company had a £100,000 overdraft. The company's affairs were confused about whether 'the wholesale system of jobbing and peculation which have so signally marked the career of Mr Hudson' would ever be broken down and identified. His liabilities were estimated at three-quarters of a million pounds, and, to mark the disfavour in which he was now held, York's Hudson Street was renamed Railway Street. *Punch* published a John Leech cartoon depicting the Railway King as a derailed locomotive. Subsequently he became a Guy Fawkes-type effigy with a paper crown being carried through the streets and jeered by noblemen, widows and Quakers.

Hudson was MP for Sunderland for fourteen years before finally and unequivocally being given his marching orders. To evade arrest for debt he went to Europe. One day in 1863, Charles Dickens, on his way home from Paris, was boarding the Folkestone packet at Boulogne, when he saw a friend, also returning to England, bidding goodbye to a poorly-dressed, ill-looking man who waved his hat from the dock forlornly as the boat pulled away. 'Surely I know that man,' said Dickens. 'I should think you do,' the friend replied. 'Hudson!'

Increasingly hard up, Hudson moved from one place to another, living in cheap lodging houses in Paris, Calais, Boulogne and Germany. When he returned home in June 1865, he astonished everyone by getting himself adopted as a general election Tory candidate for Whitby, where he found a great deal of sympathy. It was wasted. Early in the morning of Sunday, 9 July, a sheriff's officer burst into Hudson's bedroom and arrested him for debt. Protesting, he was hustled to the railway station and put on the first train to York, where he was committed to York Castle, the county jail. He flopped down in a tiny, gloomy cell where he remained for three weeks. The Tories of Whitby spent the time recruiting a local ironmaster, Charles Bagnall, to take Hudson's place as election candidate. Bagnall was duly elected. Hudson was released through the generosity of a colliery owner who paid off the Railway King's debt. The following year, at the instigation of another debtor, he was again arrested, this time outside London's Carlton Club, and taken to a debtors' prison in the City. After three weeks he was released on a legal technicality and made haste to cross the Channel once again. On 1 January 1870, however, the Abolition of Imprisonment for Debt Act became law, and Hudson could return home. At the Carlton Club he was re-elected smoking-room chairman. On a visit to York he was taken ill with angina and he travelled to London, intending to rest. Soon afterwards he had a heart attack, and, the next day, at the age of seventy-one, died, a forgotten man to the public for the past two decades. In its obituary *The Times* observed that many readers would be surprised he had remained for so long. His coffin was delivered to York for burial. By train, of course.

MOUSEMAN

Robert Thompson, a carpenter, was carving a beam on a church roof when a disgruntled colleague, brooding on the pittance they were likely to be paid, remarked that they would probably finish up as poor as church mice. Thus inspired, Thompson, on the spur of the moment, carved a tiny mouse on the beam. Years later he told his grandsons: 'I thought how a mouse manages to chew away the hardest wood, always working quietly. This was like the way it was in my workshop.' From then on Thompson regularly carved a mouse on his work. It became the most famous signature of his trade, with wooden mice scampering up clocks, creeping down table legs, crawling along chair arms, prowling on book-ends, squatting in bowls and, of course, nibbling on cheeseboards. He was the mouse world's public relations officer.

Born in 1876, Thompson was twenty when, after a spell as an apprentice with an engineering firm, he decided that his future lay

Robert Thompson's Original

with wood, specifically oak. He joined his father, a Kilburn joiner, carpenter and wheelwright, and gradually became more and more interested in carving. He also rediscovered the virtues of an ancient tool, the adze, which he wielded to give his furniture an undulating and rippled finish. His mouse arrived on the scene in 1925, three years before Mickey of that ilk made his debut. He revived a seventeenth-century style of craftsmanship, which led to appropriate commissions. A priest, for instance, asked him to make an oak cross for a figure of Christ in Ampleforth cemetery. This was followed by furniture for Ampleforth College. On four chairs he made for the Dewsbury Deaf and Dumb Society he etched sign language.

Thompson had no wish to amass great wealth, his slogan being, 'industry in quiet places', in deference to the mouse operating industriously out of the limelight. By the time he died in 1955, his work, including chairs, dividing screens, altars and lecterns, was to be seen in 700 churches up and down the country, including York Minster and Westminster Abbey.

The firm he founded has carried on over the years, producing furniture with his trademark, hand-carved mice still as popular as they were in his day. In 2000 one of the largest collections of Mouseman furniture, including oak chairs with religious motifs, lecterns, prayer desks and an altar, was sold for £24,200 at a Leeds auction.

AN INSPIRING CAT

Even as a boy Percy Shaw was a handy person to have around. Born in 1890 at Boothtown, near Halifax, he left school at thirteen, and his first job was in a blanket mill, where he carried bobbins of wool from the winders to the weavers. At evening school he learned shorthand and book-keeping, and at home he performed odd jobs like fixing new rollers on his mother's mangle. He went on to an office job, then became involved in loom construction. Other work he subsequently took on included welding and making machine tools and boilers. He invented a process for backing carpets with rubber. Though never patented, it presaged the rubber and foam-backed carpets of later years. He devised a method of re-metalling a car's big end, to save time and money. He chalked up a failure, however, with a petrol pump intended to pump anything from half a pint to twenty gallons: through leakage and evaporation, it never pumped out the amount he had put in. In the First World War he got a contract for making special wires for soldiers' khaki puttees. He also made shell noses and cartridge cases.

His first form of transport was a bicycle, but in 1916 he invested in a second-hand (or perhaps third-hand) motorised vehicle that didn't even have a kick-start. To get in he had to jump on while running alongside. On his first attempt he charged through a fence into a field, where, finding he could not stop, he had to spin round and round until he had consumed all his petrol. His first real car was a Ford Model T he called Doris, and he went on to buy and sell cars more for the love of tinkering with them than actual driving. He also became a builder of private roads and garden paths, and an expert on road surfaces.

In the evenings he would drive home along the dangerous road from Queensbury to Halifax. 'One night,' he reported, 'it was so dark I couldn't see even the tramlines. It was then that I saw some reflectors on a poster on the road and I thought it would be a good idea to bring them down to road level.' He also noticed a cat sitting on a fence, and its eyes lighting up as they reflected the poor 6-volt illumination of his headlights back to Shaw.

His ambition now was to replicate the cat's eyes, and his process was one of trial and error. First he had to find the right type of glass. He had a large variety to choose from, ranging from crude bottle glass to highly polished mirror glass. He even experimented with glass marbles set in modelling clay. Finally, in a Czech factory, he found precious samples of pure crystal glass, the sort used for expensive crystal beads and elaborate chandeliers. He was on his way.

His first road catseye was made in 1934, a veritable boon in a period when, in thick fog, tramlines were the only guide for motorists. The invention was so successful that Shaw, who was awarded an OBE, was able to buy a Rolls Royce that was neither second, nor third, hand. In 1947, during the post-war Labour government, transport minister James Callaghan set up a huge project for the installation of catseyes all over the country. Their basic design is today little changed from Shaw's original conception.

❄ ❄ ❄

BERTIE'S BOUNTY

Pontefract derives its name from two Latin words meaning 'broken bridge'. It is most famous, however, for the locally grown liquorice plants (resembling small acacia shrubs), said to have been introduced to the town by Spanish monks, who found the local soil ideal for the growth of the plants, which they enthusiastically cultivated in their monastery gardens. As early as 1614 round liquorice lozenges were being made as a cure for stomach disorders. By the end of the eighteenth century, a new industry grew up around the plant. This was the liquorice confectionery business, first located at Pontefract, where a young chemist, George Dunhill, produced sweetmeats he called Pomfret Cakes, also known as Yorkshire Pennies. In 1842, the firm of George Bassett was set up in Sheffield to produce liquorice sweets. Back in Pontefract, there were ten firms making the sweets by 1885, each with a distinctive name and shape, like Catherine Wheels, Pipes, Pencils, Bootlaces and Watches. Foremost among the Pontefract entrepreneurs was W.R. Wilkinson, whose firm is still producing millions of Pontefract Cakes, each stamped with a seal representing Pontefract's history. It depicts a monk, a castle, an owl and, of course, a broken bridge.

In 1889 a Bassett salesman, Charlie Thompson, who should be listed among the great immortals, called on a Leicester wholesaler with a sample case brimming with liquorice and cream paste specialities, like Chips (containing coconut), Rocks (bullet-shaped), Buttons (with plain jelly centres), Cubes (with five alternate layers of coloured cream paste and liquorice sheets), Nuggets (with a triple layer), plugs (plain liquorice) and Twists (twisted liquorice pieces). They were offered individually to the grim wholesaler, who refused each in turn. Charlie then clumsily gathered his sample boxes together, accidentally knocking them over and spilling the colourful sweets in a jumble on the counter. The wholesaler's eyes lit up. He saw more attraction in the 'mixed-up sweets' than in the products sold singly, and placed an order for a mixture delivery. Bassett obliged, and asked Charlie to give them a new name. He called them liquorice allsorts.

Wilkinson's is today part of the Trebor Bassett Company (Trebor being the Christian name, spelled backwards, of a founder of one of the original firms). At their factory in Sheffield forty million allsorts a week are turned out. Their emblem is Bertie Bassett, a much-loved figure, now a septuagenarian, created from allsorts.

Meanwhile Pontefract hosts an annual liquorice festival, which in 2000 included an auction of liquorice plants and presentation of such items as a sculpture of Pontefract Castle made of liquorice allsorts.

❊ ❊ ❊

A PICTURE POSTCARD PIONEER

The countenance is stern and the beard forbidding, and it is hard to discern a twinkle in the eye. It is, indeed, a picture of a typical Victorian paterfamilias. The appearance is, however, deceptive. For this is none other than James Bamforth of Holmfirth, a pioneer of the jolly picture postcard industry.

A painter and decorator's son, Bamforth had an artistic flair, an interest in photography and carpentry skills. In 1870 he launched himself into the business of producing lantern slides to accompany song and story recitals and popular lectures. He used life models and painted his own background scenery that, reportedly, could barely be distinguished from genuine moss or bracken. The models were usually his own children, staff, friends or obliging citizens he found in pub tap-rooms. For a railway episode, a bank raid or a mining disaster, outdoor photographs would be

James Bamforth
(Courtesy of Kirklees Cultural Services)

taken, mostly in the summer. Bamforth's slides were much in demand for temperance lectures, Sunday Schools, cocoa and reading-room dos and charity shows. A technical assistant would carry two cylinders of oxygen and hydrogen up and down the local hills to provide a mobile source of illumination.

The King of the Lantern Slides, as Bamforth became known, was asked to provide slides to accompany 'Billy's Rose', a tear-jerking ballad by George R. Sims, author of the verse that began, 'It is Christmas Day in the workhouse.' Bamforth's cleverly composed scenes showed drunken parents, a child's vision of 'a land of shining gold' beyond the dreary valley in which she lived, and a finale that had children meeting in heaven surrounded by angels. A harmonium would provide incidental music and sound effects. Children were paid twopence to take part in crowd scenes and a munificent fourpence if they 'starred' in a photo.

When, at the turn of the century, a Bradford firm, Riley Brothers, invested in one of the new kinematograph cameras and, crucially, a man who actually knew how to operate it, Bamforth joined them in the making of motion pictures, with son Frank as director and daughter Janie as dresser-cum-props and continuity girl. Their first efforts lasted a mere ten minutes, but were full of action, like schoolboys' snowball fights, tramps chased by policemen with large dogs, and two men trying to push each other out of a rowing boat. People in Holmfirth's main street were plastered with custard pies and drenched by fire hoses or buckets of whitewash, while constables and suffragettes performed their individual comic antics.

Bamforth's have a strong claim to be the first British firm to make films for public entertainment. They were projected by

Harry, another son, in a hired public hall while a phonograph with a large tin horn provided the music. Over the years the films developed into larger productions with professional actors, and two of Bamforth's cameramen were to become members of the Pathé Gazette newsreel team. In 1904 a new building was erected for the lantern-slide end of the business. It boasted dressing-rooms and storage space for props that included railway signal-box equipment, a ship's quarterdeck and the accoutrements of a gin palace. Six hundred titles a year were produced with a stock of two million slides.

Eventually, Bamforth's realised that picture postcards could be a new and profitable business. In 1903 one newspaper reported that in a decade Europe would be buried beneath an avalanche of cards, and Bamforth's joined in with a line illustrating pantomimes and popular songs like the Boer War favourite 'Goodbye Dolly Gray'. More decorous cards illustrated hymns and featured people well known in the town. An ideal figure for the hymn cards was one Hannah Hinchcliffe, who had a look of pure innocence and was often depicted clasping a Bible as she gazed heavenwards. She also appeared in 'kissing scenes' in comic cards.

Initially, the cards were in black and white. Later, they were thick, glossy and in colour. Eventually, Bamforth's firm had agencies in all English-speaking countries, with offices in London and New York. They employed their own artists and inevitably moved on to seaside comic cards, which constituted an empire on their own. Once regarded simply as a remote, chapel-run, textile town, Holmfirth became the hub of the most frivolous industry imaginable. When James Bamforth died in 1911, a local paper described him as 'one of Holmfirth's most honoured townsmen,' adding, 'Mr Bamforth's honourable business career stands as an example of what can be done by perseverance and honourable dealing.' Decades after his death, the world's greatest collector of picture postcards, a former American bomber pilot, built up a huge collection of Bamforth cards. Finally deciding they should be returned home, he shipped 20,000 of them across the Atlantic. They ended up in filing cabinets in Huddersfield Library.

In the course of his career Bamforth had not lacked competitors. One was Edward Dennis, who started a picture-postcard business in Scarborough in 1870. He was already producing black and white postcards when, at the end of the century, the Post Office lifted a ban on writing anything other than the address on the reverse. This paved the way for Dennis to move, like Bamforth, into colour printing, until then a Continental monopoly. His new cards featured water-colours, colour photographs and sepia prints of attractive views around the country. Many became collectors' items after a German plane, during World War II, jettisoned its bombs over Dennis' factory, destroying most of his turn-of-the-century stock. In the late 1980s the firm Dennis founded bought Bamforth's, but in 2000 it called in the receivers. The receiving order did not apply to Bamforth's which was subsequently sold to a Leeds firm, Fresh Faces, owners of a Beatles memorabilia shop in Liverpool. Fresh Faces now owns the copyright to nearly 100,000 Bamforth cards in museums and private collections.

❄ ❄ ❄

HANDSOME IS AS HANSOM DOES

Joseph Aloysius Hansom was born in October 1803, in Micklegate, York, and was only fourteen when he signed up as an apprentice with a local architect. After serving his time, he attended night-school to repair the gaps in his general education. At twenty-two, he married and moved to Halifax, where he became an architectural assistant, studying the Gothic style. Three years later, he joined an architectural partnership, becoming involved in the building of churches in Liverpool, Hull and the Isle of Man. His design of Birmingham Town Hall won a prize in a national competition, but a dispute with the builders led to his bankruptcy. On 23 December 1834, Hansom registered his idea not for a building but for a 'Patent Safety Cab', a vehicle that was to immortalise his name. The distinctive feature of the two-wheeled hansom cab was an elevated driving seat in the rear. One entered from the front through a folding door, and a seat over the axle provided room for two passengers, to whom the driver spoke through a trapdoor in the roof. Hansom disposed of his rights in the cab to a company which offered him £10,000, but of this he never received a penny. The firm got into difficulties and in 1839 Hansom temporarily took over its management to keep it running. For this service he was paid £300, the only money the cab ever earned for him. In 1842 Hansom decided that the building trade needed its own journal, and to this end founded *The Builder*, but lack of capital forced him to quit the undertaking and to rest content with a small payment from the publisher. From now on he devoted himself to church and domestic architecture. The Castle Museum in York boasts a fine example of a one-horse hansom cab.

THE CHIPPIE KING

Harry Ramsden, the man who founded an international fish and chip empire, had originally worked in a mill, as a barber's lather-boy, and, in the First World War, as an Army transport driver. After the war he opened a fish and chip shop that stayed open even on Christmas Day. There followed a second shop, after which Ramsden bought a clothing shop next door and turned it into a Cosy Café with black and white tiles and hunting prints on the walls, décor that was to become his trademark. In 1928 Harry bought, for £150, a wooden lock-up shop in White Cross, near Leeds, moving his wife and son into a nearby cottage. Three years later he built a 200-seat fish and chip restaurant across the road from the cottage. Harry was pernickety and obsessive. He insisted that it was possible to fry a fish the wrong way up. The right way was to drop it into the fat with the side from which the skin had been cut facing upwards. Then, after precisely two and a half minutes, it must be turned over and fried for another two and a half minutes. He had thermometers cut into the frying pans and issued an order that no chip could be put into the fat until the temperature registered 350 degrees Fahrenheit. He had stainless steel buckets made that carried the exact measure of chips to be cooked at any one time. Every frier carried a metal six-inch rule to check the level of the dripping, which must never be less than three and a half inches. His scales were checked daily, and he erected wooden platforms for the friers to stand on as they watched the pans. A list of 100 daily tasks that he must carry out was pinned behind a cup-

Harry Ramsden

board door. Every knife, fork and spoon bore his name, and customers filched cutlery as souvenirs of their visits to what became known as the world's biggest fish and chip shop. He found an answer to that problem. He removed his name.

Harry hired experts to devise teapots that would not drip, and introduced wall-to-wall carpets and chandeliers. One small boy was heard asking his father, 'Dad, is this where God comes for his fish and chips?' In the basement the restless Ramsden installed two snooker tables. He had gramophone records played in his office and piped to diners. The twelve figures on his front-of-house clock were replaced by the twelve letters of his name. On his rounds, one day, he spotted a plaice tail poking from a staff member's jacket pocket. He removed the tail and replaced it with fish-bits, bones and skins. From then on fish thefts came to an end. It is hardly surprising that the business Harry founded now has restaurants around the world.

BRADFORD-ON-NEVA

The Russian Revolution marked the end of a remarkable Yorkshire enterprise. On the banks of the Neva near St Petersburg, three Bradford brothers had set up what was, initially, a thriving woollen mill. It was run by Arthur and Percy Thornton and several English staff, while the third brother, Herbert, looked after the Bradford wool-buying end of the business. In Russia, it has been said, the English bosses and their families led luxurious, almost colonial lives. Would-be revolutionaries claimed that the 3,000 Russian workers were exploited. The mill compound – virtually a small town – was encircled by fencing topped by barbed wire, fitted by sympathetic Cossacks as protection against both political insurgents and marauding bears. When a British MP paid a visit, he was accompanied by armoured cars.

To investigate the mill, a young teacher, Nadezhda Krupskia, wound a kerchief round her hair to pose as a humble job-seeker and secure entrance. She claimed the conditions were appalling, and informed her fiancé, Vladimir Ilich Ulyanov, who later was to adopt the pseudonym Lenin. He harangued the workers, who then went on strike: merely the start of the Thorntons' travails.

The mill itself was imposing enough to needle a discontented proletariat. It boasted five storeys and three chimneys and was fuelled by a mixture of wood and the best Welsh coal. The six English bosses and their families lived on the top floor of an apartment block and rode around in droshkys. The mill also operated its own ferry, though, in the winter, the children could run across the frozen river.

In the compound, the Thorntons grew feed for their horses, which tugged carts bearing wool bales and chemicals from the port of St Petersburg and carried back finished cloth that went into the manufacture of army uniforms, blankets for railway travellers and tartan shawls.

One visitor to the mill was the American author Negley Farson, who was running an export business in Russia and became engaged to Arthur Thornton's daughter Vera, until she threw him over. He later claimed in *The Way of a Transgressor* that most of the Englishmen depended on hordes of servants, considering themselves 'superior as human beings to any Russian Grand Duke'. Though treated kindly, the servants were shockingly underpaid and 'regarded as clumsy St Bernards'.

In 1905 revolutionaries occupied the mill, until Cossacks took over, managing to keep a temporary peace. But over the years the workers became increasingly truculent and during the 1917 Revolution they mutinied. Caught in riots at St Petersburg (which had now become Petrograd), Farson found a cache of whisky in the cellar of the Hotel de France, and ran the gauntlet of murderous mobs to ferry the booze and an English secretary (dangerously wearing a Tsarist officer's uniform) to the mill by sleigh. There he found the Thorntons at tea: 'They might have been sitting down in Kent somewhere.'

The next day a maid rushed in crying, 'They're coming!' Nobody bothered to ask whom she meant. Thousands of Reds were swarming across the pack ice to the mill. Students in a Ford from which a red flag fluttered drove into the courtyard brandishing machine-guns. They ordered the release of the workers from their bondage. Failure to obey would result in the mill's destruction. 'All right, take them,' cried one of the Thorntons, 'and be damned.' Sensibly, his wife was more conciliatory, having tied a red band around the arm of her jumper.

The following night Arthur Thornton risked his life to help a hunted police captain escape into the forest behind the mill. Meanwhile, the workers left behind elected their own soviet, insisting on a say in the running of the mill and demanding a huge wage increase. The Thorntons yielded slowly to each demand, but realised that their Russian adventure was over.

When anarchy seemed inevitable, Farson changed his roubles for gold sovereigns, some of which went to the Thorntons and their colleagues to aid their departure from the country. Farson's leftist American friend John Reed (later to write *Ten Days That Shook The World*) guided them across the border armed with Bolshevik visas. Dorothy Shaw, thirteen-year-old daughter of one of the English staff, left with sovereigns stitched into her coat lining, while her mother carried a silver-wedding teapot. The family handed their furniture and linen to their maid. Most of the escapees fled with little more than the clothes they stood up in, some making their way through Finland and Scandinavia, others from Archangel aboard a British steamship escorted by two destroyers.

In 1918, Willie Brook, the former mill manager, submitted a £100,000 claim to the Foreign Office for assets left in Russia. He died in 1925 without recovering a penny. But in 1990 his family were awarded £3,000.

Three years later, his great-grandson, Martin Varley made a pilgrimage with his sister to St Petersburg. They found that the mill (renamed the Red Mill under Communist rule when it was run by a former shepherd) was now the Nevsky Manufacturing Factory. The façade was gaunt and some of the building's older parts had been demolished. High on a wall in the foyer Varley found a marble plaque commemorating Lenin's address. He was pleased to learn that the workers now owned shares in the firm. He was not, however, allowed to tour the building, and he and his sister had to be content with buying woollen goods from the mill shop.

❊ ❊ ❊

THE ROADS THAT JACK BUILT

Despite his infirmity Blind Jack Metcalf of Knaresborough became one of the eighteenth century's outstanding road-builders. He was also probably the only blind soldier in military history.

Sightless since the age of six, after an attack of smallpox, he spent much of his boyhood birds'-nesting, guided by friends' voices. Years later he rode to hounds and was an expert swimmer, fond of diving for objects dropped in the local River Nidd. He once made an attempt to rescue a farm worker swept into a pool while trying to save a cow trapped underwater by a huge boulder. By an almost superhuman effort Blind Jack recovered the man, but too late to save his life.

Metcalf was also a proficient violinist, having mastered fifty tunes while still a young boy. He was playing for dancers at the Royal Oak, Harrogate, when he met the love of his life, Dolly Benson, the landlord's daughter. Unfortunately, her mother had forced her to become engaged to a shoemaker. Dolly accordingly placed a ladder against the inn wall, enabling Metcalf to climb up, tap on her window, and accompany her to the ground. They made off and wed the next morning. They bought a cottage and had four daughters. Jack ran a horse-drawn taxi service to and from the Harrogate Pump Room, and later, using pack horses, fetched fish from the Yorkshire coast across the moors in all weathers, to be sold to eager housewives.

Then came military service, during which he survived the English defeat following the Forty-Five Rebellion. He played his fiddle to encourage his countrymen when they turned the tables on the Jacobites at Culloden. Why had he been accepted as a recruit in the first place? Probably because of his size. His height has been reported as anything from six feet three to seven feet three. His walking stick, displayed today in a glass case in Knaresborough Castle, confirms he was unusually tall.

On his demobilisation, he resumed the trade of carrier, and while driving a stage-wagon between York and Harrogate realised how bad the local roads were. He succeeded in getting a contract for the repair of a three-mile stretch between Harrogate and Boroughbridge, making use of his Viameter, a strange contraption he was said to have invented himself. Also to be seen in

Blind Jack Metcalf in his seventies

Knaresborough Castle, it is a wooden wheel circled by an iron tyre with a handle, gripping which the operator could trundle it over the ground to assess the nature of the surface. Between the wheel and the handle is a dial, each rotation of whose pointer Metcalf could check as it touched his fingertip, to measure the distance covered.

Metcalf was assigned increasing numbers of road-building jobs. The hardest, in 1759, was the creation of twenty-one miles of road from Wakefield to Huddersfield, thence over Crosland Moor to Marsden, and from there over the 1,250-foot Standedge hill on the way to Manchester. At some points an army of 400 men was employed. When they reached a marsh or bog, they would lay stout bundles of heather and gorse on which they placed stones that would tolerate the passage of pedestrians, horses and wagons. Carrying most of his calculations in his head, Metcalf is said to have built a total of 180 miles of road, often over the most difficult terrain. He also constructed bridges. He retired at seventy-five and died at ninety-two.

❄ ❄ ❄

THE MAN WHO DIDN'T CARE FOR MOVIES

J. Arthur Rank wasn't all that enamoured of movies, or, for that matter, the people who appeared in them. As a gun-dog breeder, he once said: 'I named all the dogs after generals and the bitches after movie stars.' His cynicism, perhaps, could be ascribed to his down-to-earth Yorkshire upbringing.

Rank was born in 1888 at Pearson Park, Hull, in a house since demolished. The youngest of seven children, he was taught at a Cambridge school by the master who was to become the model for the central character of *Goodbye Mr Chips* (with the film of which Arthur had no connection). His father had made a fortune in the flour-milling business and gave much of it away to the Methodist movement. He passed his religious fervour on to Arthur, who taught at the Sunday School of the Methodist Church in Queens Road, Hull.

Arthur began his career at seventeen sweeping the floors in his father's mills, working his way up until he was familiar with every aspect of the business. During the First World War he was an ambulance driver in France. A year after the war ended, his father gave him a million pounds, stating, 'There won't be any more after I'm gone.' Following an unhappy spell with a self-raising flour firm, he rejoined the family business.

He became attracted to film as a medium for spreading the gospel, first screening films for his Sunday School class, and going on to produce his own religious films. The first movie he made for the general public was *Turn of the Tide* in 1935, a moralistic tale of a feud between two fishing families which ends in marriage, described by Graham Greene as 'an unpretentious and truthful film'. Within a few years Rank was in control of most of the British film industry, involved in production, distribution and exhibiting. He took over Denham, Pinewood and Islington studios and the Gaumont-British and Odeon cinema circuits. The Rank Organisation sustained the Archers, Two Cities and Cineguild production companies, and the stars linked with Rank made up almost the entire cast of the British cinema. The half-naked man striking a gong before the title credits became a familiar symbol of the all-pervading Rank empire. As it grew, so did his charity work. He is thought to have given away £100 million during his lifetime. But he loved his flour-milling business – which became known as Rank Hovis McDougall – better than any studio.

CHAPTER 10

MOBS

SAVE OUR BODIES

Among the more estimable citizens of nineteenth-century Leeds were two doctors, Charles Thackrah and Robert Baker. Both were social reformers, campaigning for improvements in living and working conditions. Thackrah wrote a book describing the horrors of industrial labour, and set up his own medical school. Baker became one of the country's first factory inspectors and produced a cholera map indicating those areas of Leeds in which it was most dangerous to live. The two men, however, were also involved in an extracurricular activity. They were resurrectionists, or, in simpler language, body-snatchers, using the corpses they stole to aid their researches. Thackrah would send out his own students on church-yard forays to unearth bodies. He himself posted his wife as a look-out while he was busy digging in a Leeds burial ground. After one of Baker's body-snatching expeditions, relatives of the deceased whose remains had been filched put up posters pleading for the body's return. In favour of the two doctors it has to be said that all this happened at a time when body-snatching was rife. Earlier surgeons had bought the bodies of hanged felons for dissection purposes. This was even regarded as a form of post-mortem punishment.

In the winter of 1832 a Parliamentary election was held in Leeds, and a big political issue was the recently passed Anatomy Act, which aimed at discouraging the general practice of snatching bodies and encouraging the purchase of the bodies of people who had died in workhouses for dissection purposes. The Leeds Workhouse trustees welcomed the Act and appointed a committee to oversee the distribution of workhouse bodies – 'the friendless poor' – to anatomists in the city. There was a public furore among those who claimed that the poor were now to be treated with signal contempt, having no say in the disposal of their own bodies. One public speaker declared: 'Let them act under a measure which dispenses equal justice to all – the rich as well as the poor – the fat sinecurist as well as the worn-out labourer, and then, when all are equally dealt with, they might talk as much as they please about the necessities of science.' (Loud cheers.)

Until 1832, Leeds had been unrepresented in Parliament and civic politics were thus considered of great importance. For the election there were two Liberal candidates, the historian Thomas Babington Macaulay, who had sponsored the Anatomy Act, and a local man, the son of a rich flax-maker John Marshall, jun. Their opponent was Michael Sadler, leader of a Tory–Radical alliance, on record as being against the exploitation of the poor, alive or dead. On nomination day rival processions lined up in the streets. In Sadler's parade were workers carrying banners, one of which was to cause consternation at the Home Office and fury in the conservative medical press. It depicted a skeleton on a black background with a yellow (for Liberal) border. In its right hand the skeleton clutched a scroll ironically inscribed, 'Anatomy Bill to better the condition of the helpless poor'. Beneath were the words, 'Macaulay and the Anatomy Bill'. The skeleton not only represented Macaulay without his fine clothes, but was the very personification of Death. As one historian later wrote, it metaphorically dissected Macaulay just as he himself would be responsible for inflicting dissection on the poor. At the hustings there was turmoil. Some Liberal supporters made violent attempts to snatch and destroy the banner. But it was well defended, and they were beaten off.

Sadler lost the poll, and his working-class supporters expressed their dismay by burning effigies of Macaulay and Marshall in the streets. Doctors who had marched in Sadler's procession were vilified in the *London Medical Gazette* as a disgrace to their profession.

TOLL-BOOTH TERROR

Road tolls, which involved the setting up of payment booths and the blocking of highways, led, in 1753, to an outburst of rage. Mobs from Yeadon and Otley joined forces and smashed a dozen toll bars with hatchets. At Selby the public bellman urged citizens to torch or hack down a toll bar. The worst fighting was in Leeds, where a large body of armed rioters marched to Harewood Bridge, where a turnpike had been erected. The owner of Harewood Estate assembled his own army and arrested thirty men, later imprisoned. When the angry crowd attacked again, soldiers were summoned from York. The rioters gathered outside the Old King's Arms in Leeds and hurled stones and bricks at the military. The soldiers fired back and eight rioters were shot dead and forty wounded.

❄ ❄ ❄

NO JABS!

Even today vaccination against disease can be a controverisal topic. In the 1870s it caused a riot. The seeds of the disturbance were sown when the Keighley Board of Guardians, responsible for running the town's affairs, announced its opposition to the new Vaccination Acts which required all small children to be immunised against smallpox. The Board feared that the practice, then in its infancy, was dangerous and could be the cause of other diseases. Disturbing cases had been reported that lent credence to their claim.

In their wisdom, the Guardians set up the Keighley District Anti-Compulsory Vaccination League. A speech recorded in one of their minute books read:

> We must strike now or never. Each one of us must work as if the whole of the proof lay on our shoulders. Do not let it be said that the town was backward or weak-kneed. The committee should be urged to seek out cases of injury, instances of any children being boycotted by schools, or youths, male or female, who have been refused

as pupil teachers for neglect of vaccination. In the interests of liberty, in the interests of our children's health, I beg of you not to delay this.

Membership of the new society soared.

The Government hit back, authorising magistrates to order the arrest of persons who failed to appear when summoned for non-compliance with the new law. They should inflict fines of up to a pound. One of the League's cash-books reveals that hundreds of such fines were indeed imposed. When the Guardians themselves were threatened with imprisonment for contempt of court, they merely intensified their campaign, hiring supportive speakers from all over Yorkshire. A solicitor was also engaged and tracts were printed under such titles as 'Death to Vaccination', which, according to posters plastered around the town, was simply a means of putting one shilling and sixpence per person into the public vaccinator's pocket. The Guardians sent congratulatory letters to parents who refused to have their children vaccinated. Boiling point was reached on 10 August 1876, with the arrest of J. Jeffrey, one of the Guardians. His colleagues were picked up the next day, while their workmates booed the arresting officers. One Guardian tracked down to his farm turned to his wife and said, 'I hope the sheriff's men will be vaccinated twice every morning and once every night as long as they live.' Another Guardian simply refused to walk with the officers who called for him. They grabbed him and, with not too much difficulty, hustled him away.

The sheriff's posse led the prisoners to the Devonshire Hotel (now the Grinning Rat) for a meal before catching the train to York, where they were to be locked away. Thousands of mill workers who had finished their shifts surrounded the building. The doors were locked against them, but the men fought their way into the courtyard. They kicked and stoned a policeman, and even the superintendent in charge of the operation was treated roughly. Attempting to escape, the officers thrust their prisoners onto a horse-drawn omnibus. The crowd ripped its top off, unharnessed the horses and dragged the bus, officers and Guardians through the town. 'Where are we going?' one scared officer asked. 'To the beck,' was the answer. Luckily, no one was drowned.

When a local auctioneer tried to make peace between the warring parties, the mob attacked him. As he ran into the Mechanics Institute, his coat was torn off and the building's windows smashed. One elderly officer collapsed and was escorted into the Hare and Hounds (now an Abbey National office). Two prisoners broke free, dashed into a house, climbed upstairs, threw open the bedroom windows and made victory speeches. For good measure, the auctioneer's office was vandalised.

The following day those prisoners still in custody were paraded into the sheriff's office, each carrying a carpet bag. They were taken to the station and pushed into the York train. As it got up steam, one shouted, 'We are standing for God and the right.' The assembled crowd roared: 'Stand firm!'

Imprisoned in York Castle, the Guardians found they had attained the status of martyrs. Their cells had been whitewashed and their bedclothes were fresh. They were treated to extra food and a chess set, tobacco, grapes, books and cash.

On 8 September they were released on bail, and, on returning to Keighley, were greeted as heroes as they stood on a wagon accompanied by two brass bands. But when they were tried in London, they swore not to interfere with the new legislation, and from then on the movement they had led fizzled out.

❅ ❅ ❅

CAPTURE HUDDERSFIELD!

On a day in February 1812, a gang of men with faces blackened to conceal their identities forced their way into a Huddersfield mill and, after smashing all the machinery, tore the building down. Two days later soldiers were moved to the scene, but, despite their presence, a similar attack was launched on a second mill later the same month. There was 'great alarm' in the town, the *Leeds Mercury* reported. A meeting of factory bosses was convened at which several special constables were sworn in and a reward of 100 guineas offered for the apprehension of anyone who had taken part in these outrages. The public, however, were uncooperative, proving they were solidly behind the machine breakers. On the evening of Sunday 21 March, several armed men assembled outside a mill, announcing their arrival by firing a pistol. Here they broke thirty pairs of shears, and burned raw wool and fine cloth on a stove. Though they styled themselves Luddites, they were opposed less to the installation of machines than to unpopular employers. At the St Crispin Inn in Halifax, headquarters of a group who supported the French Revolution, plans were laid to spread their activities to the Spen Valley. Special preparations were made to attack a Heckmondwike mill whose owner was notoriously harsh. Meanwhile the Luddites were becoming increasingly sophisticated in their organisation, exacting subscriptions to finance their operations. But when they made their assault, they found the owner fully prepared. On duty were at least nine armed guards and a watchdog, while troops were billeted at nearby inns. The mill's gates and inner doors had been heavily fortified and reinforced with iron bars. Spikes eighteen inches long lined the staircase, and at the head of the stairs stood a huge carboy of vitriol, ready for pouring over the rioters. In three ranks the Luddites moved in. Those in the front rank brandished pistols, while the second rank waved hatchets and the third gripped hammers suitable for machine smashing. Shattering windows, they fired into the mill. The shots roused the guards and an alarm bell clanged. A twenty-minute battle ensued, but, having failed to break down the main doors, the attackers retreated. The next morning, several hammers, axes, two masks and 'a powder horn with a bullet mould', according to the *Leeds Mercury*, were found in 'a field which was stained in several places with blood'. The wounded were carried to Roberttown, where onlookers were clearly sympathetic to their cause.

Government spies eager to extract information about the ringleaders were greeted by a wall of silence from citizens who, it was claimed, had already helped many men to escape and given them food and shelter. On 18 April, the mill boss came to Huddersfield for the trial of a soldier who had refused to fire on the rioters. As he made his way home later, an unsuccessful attempt was made to murder him. Antipathy to the boss, a Mr Cartwright, remained strong, even among the middle classes and tradespeople. This became abundantly clear when thirteen pairs of shears Cartwright had sent to Huddersfield for sharpening were returned in pieces. To revive their prestige, the machine breakers realised they needed to mount a massive operation against a local manufacturer. Their chosen victim was the extremely unpopular William Horsfall, who had already introduced new machinery into his cropping shop, thus antagonising the hand-croppers, who linked up to form a Luddite group. Like Cartwright, Horsfall had taken precautions to protect his mill but was careless about his personal safety. It was therefore concluded that an attempt on his life would be less dangerous than an assault on the mill, and would create more publicity for the cause. The attempt was made as he returned from Huddersfield's George Hotel to the mill at Ottiwells, near Slaithwaite. Four men with horse pistols suddenly appeared, shot him fatally and disappeared into a wood. All were masked and wore dark, coarse woollen coats. A £2,000 reward was offered for information.

There was now talk of a general uprising, and the local Luddites amassed arms, which they hid in a depot of whose location the soldiery remained ignorant. Large bodies of men were often seen at night performing military-style exercises, and several lead vessels were stolen to be melted down into bullets. On 1 June, the Government spies denounced several local men as Luddites, notably James Oldroyd of Dewsbury, who had been involved in the abortive attack on Cartwright's mill. Such was local support that Oldroyd was able to provide an alibi that satisfied his trial jury, even though a spy gave evidence on oath against him. He was freed. A man named Baines, leader of the Halifax Luddites and of the St Crispin Republican Club was also denounced by spies who had infiltrated his organisation, but it took two men to swear to his guilt before a jury would convict. The Luddites now went underground and, from their point of view, the murder of Horsfall proved successful as his mill machines were removed.

A man was then arrested who gave a local magistrate 'the most complete satisfactory evidence' relating to the murder. He said that when the killer saw him, 'he changed colour and gasped for breath'. After hearing the informer's evidence, he exclaimed, 'Damn that fellow. He has done me.' He was George Mellor, leader of the Huddersfield Luddites from the day of their formation in a cropping shop. The informer was Benjamin Walker, who had been his chief accomplice, but had turned King's Evidence for the £2,000 reward. Thanks to Walker, the other two men involved in the murder, William Thorpe and Thomas Smith, were arrested. Other arrests followed, and before the year's end sixty-four were imprisoned in York Castle. Though the leaders were now in custody, isolated incidents continued, including the attempted murder of a key witness. At the York trial the chief witnesses were Walker, three men who saw the murder, the surgeon who attended Horsfall, the man with whom the trusting Mellor had left his gun after the attack, and the wife of Mellor's cousin, with whom he had sought refuge after the murder. All three were convicted, sentenced to death and executed in less than a week. With their deaths, local Luddism lost much of its impetus. But unrest was not at an end.

After 1815 the privations caused by the economic dislocation following the Napoleonic wars caused fresh disturbances. On 16 August 1819 – the same day as the Peterloo Massacre in Manchester – Huddersfield's cloth workers met in a field and conceived an ambitious plan: nothing less than the storming of the town. This came to nothing when news leaked of the readiness of the military to deal with such an insurgence, and the would-be attackers dispersed. But the scheme was not forgotten, and in 1820 there was an attempt to capture the town and take local magistrates as hostages, signalling the start of a nationwide revolt. After the lighting of a beacon on Castle Hill, four contingents marched to an old Luddite meeting place. They were seen by travellers on the Leeds–Huddersfield road, who reported the event on arrival in Huddersfield. The magistrates called a public meeting and put emergency laws into operation. Shops were closed, barricades erected and townsfolk armed. When the malcontents marched into the town, they would have outnumbered the troops and armed citizens, and would easily have taken it over, but on receiving misinformation from their own informers, they fled back to their villages. Huddersfield was saved.